...hroughout his... colleges and universities. He holds... and psychology and has contributed widely to academic books and journals. He is retired and lives with his wife, Catherine, and two male Maine Coon cats, Luis and Max, in a remote country cottage in Northumberland.

Also by Denis O'Connor

Paw Tracks in the Moonlight
Paw Tracks at Owl Cottage

Paw Tracks

A Childhood Memoir

Denis O'Connor

Constable • London

Constable & Robinson Ltd
55–56 Russell Square
London WC1B 4HP
www.constablerobinson.com

First published in the UK by Constable,
an imprint of Constable & Robinson Ltd, 2012

A copy of the British Library Cataloguing in
Publication data is available from the British Library

ISBN: 978-1-84901-997-2 (paperback)
ISBN: 978-1-78033-016-7 (ebook)

Printed and bound by CPI Group (UK) Ltd, Croydon, CR0 4YY

1 3 5 7 9 10 8 6 4 2

This book is for my grandchildren.

I gratefully acknowledge the tremendous support and love from my wife Catherine, which has sustained and nurtured me throughout the writing of this book.

I will a round unvarnished tale deliver.

William Shakespeare, *Othello*

CONTENTS

Awakening   1

A Glimpse Through the Trees   3

Back to the Beginning   19

Sojourn from Trouble   39

A Wildcat in Scotland   59

A Family Affair   73

Friends in the Park   87

The White Cat   103

A Terrifying Dog Called Bruno   117

A Bicycle at Last   129

The Final Beating   143

Attack at the Stables   155

Wildfire   167

Taking Flight   197

AWAKENING

One morning I saw the most beautiful rainbow I had ever seen and that day became even more unusual when I was visited by a colourful and charming little bird. I had climbed the backyard wall in the terraced street of houses where we then lived. It was raining but despite that I wanted a better view of the rainbow whose vibrant colours lit up the sky and filled me with such joy that I hoped it would stay there forever. I was eight years old. My mother came out into the yard and called for me to come down before I caught cold. Just then, seemingly out of nowhere, a blue tit, a bird which I had only seen on a chart in school, landed on my sleeve and stayed there. For a long moment we looked at each other, this tiny, exquisitely coloured bird and I, and then, to my disappointment, it flew away. It had been only a few passing seconds but somehow it seemed that the bird and the rainbow were related in their significance. It was as if they had appeared for me alone on what was an otherwise gloomy, rain-filled day. I kept the memory of those moments alive in my mind.

That night, whilst I lay sleepless in bed, the images of the rainbow and the bird came back and they now assumed the aura of messengers. It would take me a long time to unravel the message they had been sent to give me but, in the darkness of my bedroom that night, I already felt that those images held an exciting promise, a tale of contact with natural-born creatures which would become part of my destiny. I knew that the only thing that I could do was to follow that blue tit, the harbinger of the way to follow, through the woods to where wildlife flourished, where I would learn from the birds and other wild creatures who dwelled free within the bounties that nature provided. It was as if the core of me was waking up: I knew I would have to strive hard to nurture this part of me that hadn't yet matured, but it would lead me to the place I really belonged, possibly somewhere beautiful. But for now it was all simply the hint of a dream as yet undefined. I guessed that the bird was not likely to frequent our backyard ever again, and I never did see another brilliant rainbow over the wall. But nature had already delivered its message, which would lead me, over many years of questing, finally to Owl Cottage.

A GLIMPSE THROUGH THE TREES

I had found a place in the woods. It was a secret place. It was my place. It was a place where I could be me, with neither constraints nor controls except the laws of nature. Here I was truly in my element and no one could find me. I could sit on a log stump for hours with only the company of the wild things around me. For an eight-year-old going on nine this place had all the possibilities of exciting adventures as well as offering a safe refuge from my world of fear and repression.

The place I had found was enveloped in greenery with only needlepoints of sunlight glinting through the tree foliage overhead as it swayed gently in tune with a soft summer breeze. The stray sunbeams warmed me, as if they were stroking and comforting me. Here, alone and quiet, deep in the woods with my senses finely tuned to the natural surroundings, I soon became aware of a throbbing and humming that was the life force of nature itself, a sound that can be heard only if you listen very carefully and perhaps only if you are young and sensitive enough. As I became aware of the deep rhythms of nature, I could feel the ground breathe beneath my feet as if its heart was beating in harmony with the turning of the earth. It was truly magical and I was thrilled to be the silent witness of this inspiring moment and I marvelled at its wonder. As I was taking it all in,

I too became the subject of scrutiny as the denizens of the wild wood inspected my presence, simply out of their curiosity and need for survival. Here and there, from within the shadowy shade of the bushes and tall stem grasses, a disparate company of small creatures watched me. They saw me but I only caught sight of what might have been an eye, brown and luminous, possibly a rabbit or a hare, peeping from within the thick cover of undergrowth. Birds began to appear and viewed me with quick darting inquisitive glances as they flitted from one slim perch to another. They were nervous in their proximity to me, but were still confident that at the least hint of threat they could vanish into thin air. A robin, bolder than the rest of the feathered colony, settled close by and, cocking his head from side to side, gave me a probing stare. In a tall beech tree high above me but out of my sight I could hear the raucous calls of the rooks who knew where I was and were puzzled as to what I was doing there. Little happens in the wild wood without their knowledge and they are ever vigilant against the menace posed by outsiders.

Now and then something moved in the undergrowth and I barely glimpsed dark silhouettes moving around the periphery of my location. An especially large shape emerged to reveal a mature roe deer, a doe who quite possibly had a fawn hidden nearby. She stared directly at me and I could sense the primeval fear that held her rigid and ready to bolt. She beheld me, despite my youth, as the enemy, Man, whose kind regularly hunted her breed to death. I was an intruder, not welcome here in this place that belonged to the wild ones that lived free among the trees and by the streams that fed the lake. The doe's wide-eyed stare and stance broadcast this message clearly to me. But I wanted – I yearned and desired with all my young heart – to be accepted as part of what was there. I felt that I, too, belonged in this place. I devoutly wished to become a member of my adopted wildlife family.

I had nowhere else to go where I could feel safe and secure. To be here gave me a feeling of contentment that I could not find anywhere else. In this private space, time seemed suspended: I didn't have to worry about what had just happened at home or school, or get anxious about what would happen tomorrow. Only here could I defer thinking about common-place things and open my mind to what I thought were universal truths. I could feel these thoughts, so much bigger than me, slyly slipping into my awareness like a balm to soothe as well as excite my intellect. I began to realize that something was happening to me: my burgeoning devotion to nature was in some way being reciprocated. In return for my whole-hearted attachment, nature was giving me gifts of insight and wisdom. The bringers of those gifts were the living things surrounding me. The trees, the flowers, the birds and the animals, even the butterflies – every living thing that nature had endowed with sentient knowledge – were teaching me. They were the agents of my intuition and I was being educated discreetly through my senses. Here as I was, sitting deep in meditation beneath the shelter of a tree, a little boy emulating Buddha and starting to absorb knowledge as life intended.

As I heeded the thoughts invading my mind I was inspired with the knowledge that nature was a force for change but that it was more subtle than destructive: it could help us improve ourselves. It helps to marshal all the resources afforded to every creature to strive to be something better – to adapt and improve, adjust to what is possible and make the most of not only what you are but what you can become. Improve and change was nature's clarion call and I was learning this, not in school, but here in the sanctuary of the wild wood. In my hiding place my fears were calmed, the confusion of my young life was quietened down. This state of repose allowed me to think about who I was and about my place in the world for the first time.

One thing that first occurred to me there amongst the quiet hubbub of nature was a realization that, as a human, I wasn't superior to all the animals around me. The life of even the humblest little animal was just as important to itself as my life was to me. I realized that this is nature's essential law, and later in my life learned about the Gaia hypothesis in which the earth is seen as a single living organism, so we should treat all aspects of the planet with the love and respect we give to ourselves. If we hurt and damage the earth, then we hurt and damage ourselves.

Soon, too soon, it would be time for me to leave and return to my life at home and with that realization I felt the onset of dread at what awaited me there.

6

When I was at home I felt like I was a prisoner subject to inflexible rules and obliged to accept a dogma which was anathema to me. My family lived in a strange atmosphere of oppression. My father, Bernard O'Connor, was the son of a large Irish immigrant family of eight brothers and four daughters. He was the second youngest child of the family; his brother Dan was the youngest. He was an ardent Roman Catholic in keeping with the fervent Irish Catholicism of his family. My mother, Isabelle née Watson, became a Catholic as a condition of her marriage to my father. I had two younger sisters, Brenda and Gloria, and we all lived in a small terraced house with only two bedrooms at No. 30, Mary Street, in Blaydon-upon-Tyne, County Durham. This oppression took the form of an emotional straitjacket that restricted what would have been considered just ordinary behaviour in almost any other household. The overbearing presence hanging over all of us was an angry and judgemental God. Almost all inclinations, desires and even thoughts were deemed sinful. And because this view was perpetually impressed upon us by our parents, especially by my father, we children lived in a constant state of self-condemnation. I struggled against this and was regularly punished physically for allegedly offending God.

In the small, cramped house where we all lived, personal privacy was limited but if you saw something you shouldn't have it was better to look away and pretend you hadn't seen it. Modesty was carried to extremes to the extent that to take a peek at one's own body was frowned upon. Inhibitions were the order of the day and freedom of expression in any form was forbidden. There were no books allowed except the Bible and prayer books, which we were often given as presents. Children's comics were allowed, as well as a few hardbound comic annuals but classical literature was banned just to be on the safe side of extreme Christian morality. Junior school professed a broadly similar outlook and the teachers, especially the men, wielded the rod with gusto so that no child would be 'spoiled'.

I struggled against the harshness of this way of life both at home and at school and was regularly beaten for my disobedience. At home, if I made a noise playing, sang a song out loud or grumbled at having to join in family prayer sessions, my father would hit me across the head and face – boxing my ears, he called it. At school, if I was unable to answer correctly a question from the catechism, a small book of Catholic dogma, or if I laughed or made a mistake in my maths book, I was caned on the hand by a teacher. I grew to hate my life and hate is a rabid soul-destroyer when it is unspoken and kept tight inside.

By the time I was eight and found my hiding place in the woods, this hatred had already persisted for a long time. It had even affected my general well-being to the extent that I began to look sickly and withdrawn. I was unhappy and afraid, and sometimes these feelings caused me to vomit my food back up and often induced bouts of breathlessness. In my weakened state, I was also prone to infections and confined to bed with diseases such as measles and chicken pox. Adults would often accuse me of looking pale and miserable, but nobody knew if there was something seriously wrong with me.

I was taken to see the doctor, who suspected that the root of my problems were not really physical and referred me to the city hospital for the attention of a psychologist. I remember talking to a lady in a white coat who asked me a lot of questions, most of which I felt unable to answer. I was terrified in case the doctors would lock me up in hospital if I did not improve, which is what my father threatened would happen.

My father muttered that it was all a waste of time and we took the bus home. In the evening, whilst we were alone at home, he berated me for causing the family trouble and shame. I did not dare answer him back as I knew full well that if I did he would hit me. I remember thinking about running away. After poking the fire he laid the hot poker against my leg and snarled, 'There's something for you to really sniffle about.'

I was shocked and started to cry but my tears were ignored.

When my mother returned from a night out visiting friends he explained there had been an accident. He glared at me and I didn't dare tell my mother the truth. For such an avid religious man he often proved to be a clever liar. I thought that if I did not keep quiet he would take me back to the hospital to have me locked up or would even kill me. I did not want to leave my mother so I held my tongue.

The pain in my leg that night in bed was so severe that I wept and could not sleep. The following morning my mother summoned the doctor who sprinkled some kind of powder on the burn and fastened a thick bandage around it. It took a month before it healed over with a lumpy, angry-looking red scar. While it was healing, the pain made me limp, which made some of the school kids scoff and laugh at me, calling me a cripple. From that point onwards, I started truanting from school to hide in the woods and my mother, grandmother and other caring relatives became even more concerned about my lack of well-being and the nervous state I was in.

Acting on an instinctive, caring impulse, my Aunt Kathleen presented me with a surprise gift, a puppy dog. This act of kindness changed my life for the better and, as it transpired, forever. The puppy was a crossbred little mongrel with some black and white sheepdog in him and he was the first real friend I ever had. It was 1942 and the Second World War was still raging so I called him Monty after General Bernard Montgomery, the war hero. True to his canine species, Monty showered me with love and devotion from the onset of our relationship and in return I worshipped him. We became instantly inseparable. It is not surprising that dogs have been called man's best friend, as I found out with Monty. He made it plain that I belonged to him and that he belonged to me – he seemed to think it was his good fortune to be my dog. We played together all day long when I was not in school and I laughed and laughed at his puppy antics. He made me feel happy and excited about life and I smothered him with cuddles to show how much I loved him.

I suddenly realized what I had been missing was something to love and to be loved by in return. This dog had brought me release from all the twisted hurt – all that emotional baggage – that I was carrying around from such an early age. It seemed to me that his entry into my life was a kind of salvation. His evident love for me made me start to change. I began to like myself. I begged my mother to allow me to let him sleep on my bed. But guess what? He did a pee on the counterpane and all hell broke loose. My father, who was not well disposed towards me at any time, blamed me and ordered the puppy to be confined to the backyard for the rest of the freezing-cold night. And then, knotting a towel several times, he beat me with it, while calling me stupid and useless. I bore the beating without crying because I had found previously that bawling and blubbering only made him more violent towards me. I could hear my mother weeping in the next door room. Rather than worrying about myself, I was more concerned about what was happening to Monty who I could hear whining in the yard below.

After the beating, I lay awake listening until the house had fallen silent. I didn't dare switch on the bedside lamp that my grandmother had bought for me in case it alerted my father but I lit a stump of candle I kept on the mantelpiece. Then I sneaked barefoot downstairs and let my puppy back in. Shushing him to be silent, I took him with me up to my bedroom. He seemed to understand only too well the need to be quiet and snuggled into me for warmth and comfort. He only gave an occasional whimper of self pity as he started to warm up after his ordeal in the cold backyard. I blew out the candle. The darkness of the night in my bedroom was all enveloping and it shrouded us in safety as long as we were still and mute. It was my fervent hope that we would escape detection until my father, a joiner working for the Co-operative stores, left for work early next morning. In truth, I didn't care if I was punished again because in my mind I had done the right thing and my puppy was safe beside me. Our bodies warmed each other as we cuddled up and we soon fell fast asleep.

The companionship of Monty caused an awakening in me which opened a multitude of opportunities for joyous living. We went everywhere together except to school and church. At four o'clock every weekday afternoon Monty would be waiting for me at the school gates. We had great fun together romping in the fields and by the banks of the River Tyne. We would run wildly as if we had wings on our feet and Monty would leap at my legs to knock me over and we would wrestle together like bear cubs at play. I fashioned sticks for him from fallen branches with my clasp knife, a gift from my Uncle John who was a scout master, and when I tossed them high and away he would race with all the energy in him to catch and retrieve them. One day my grandmother gave me sixpence after running an errand for her and I bought two threepenny bags of chips with batter bits. Monty and I ran up to the Summer Hill Field and ate our chips there. I chuckled as I watched my dog chewing the chips and crunching the batter with such obvious relish. Living with Monty felt good – he was the best thing that had ever happened in my life. Nothing I had felt before compared to being with him. For the first time in a long time I was suffused with happiness.

I remember, all too clearly, a Friday near the end of July. The sun was shining as school finished for the holidays. I had lots of plans for the carefree weeks ahead when Monty and I could be together all the time. As the caretaker opened the huge gates to allow the children out I expected to see Monty waiting for me as usual. I was really looking forward to seeing him and I was in high spirits. Only, he wasn't there. I ran out in the street and looked everywhere for him but there was no sign of him. I called his name several times but he didn't appear.

Oh well, I thought, perhaps he got locked in the yard and my mother wasn't there to let him go because he certainly knew the time I finished school and was always prompt. I burst into the backyard, calling his name, but he was nowhere to be seen. My mother was busy at the kitchen bench preparing vegetables for dinner and in response to my eager questions she did not turn to face me and simply said, 'He must have gone out earlier.'

Just to make sure he wasn't in the house I ran upstairs and looked in my bedroom. No Monty. I ran out into the street and began a desperate search for him, anywhere and everywhere. It is strange how the mind works when you've lost something because you look in the most unlikely places. And so it was in my search for Monty. It seemed as if he had disappeared from the face of the earth. Eventually I borrowed a bike from a girl who lived down the street and I extended the hunt ever wider. I looked for him until it grew dark and I could hardly see, by which time it was very late. When I returned home my mother and sisters were in bed and there was just my father waiting for me. I was severely told off for being out so late but, strangely, he didn't beat me. I hastened to bed hungry, but also worried and frightened at what might have happened to my dog.

For three weeks I looked everywhere for him. I even checked the police station and the Dog and Cat's Rescue Shelter in Scotswood. Monty could just not be found. I could not believe how totally he had vanished and thought that he must have been stolen. This belief comforted me because I was sure that one day I would find him again. I was sure that we would immediately recognize each other and all would be well.

Then one day I was talking about Monty to my sixteen-year-old cousin Billy. Even though he was much older than me, he often came to see me. He had shown me how to spin a cricket ball and said he would teach me how to play billiards when I was older. He turned to me and told me to forget about Monty.

'Stop wasting your time looking for him, he's long gone,' he said. 'You'll never find him. Your dad thought you were spending too much time with him, missing church services and wasting your time with a dog and so he took him to the vet's and had him put to death.'

As the significance of Billy's words penetrated my brain I started whirling around in a macabre dance of denial and horror. There and then I suffered a sudden and severe attack of agony and distress. I began to tremble with the trauma of realizing that my Monty had been taken from me and executed for nothing but the whim of a cruel man. The pain was unbearable. I felt like I had been broken into pieces and that life would never be the same again.

Sheer terror took hold of me and I fled. I didn't know where I was running to – I just ran and my mind subconsciously directed me to the only place where I could find refuge and peace. It had started to rain heavily and by the time I reached the outskirts of Axwell Park Woods I was in a state of collapse and drenched to the bone. I sought and found oblivion and collapsed into the undergrowth between trees and dense bushes. I wanted to die. The pouring rain chilled me into an icy sleep that would have been terminal had it not been for the chance intervention of a young golden retriever, called Goldie, who sniffed me out in the darkness. Her wild howls and frantic barking at my plight alarmed all the householders in the neighbouring parkland and brought help running towards me. Later, it seemed to me quite amazing that I been brought near to death by the loss of my dog, Monty, but my life was in turn saved by the intervention of another dog that I had never seen before.

I was rushed to the local hospital at Whickham where a severe condition of hyperthermia developed into a raging fever, which was followed by double pneumonia. The medical prognosis was doubtful that I would live another forty-eight hours but the staff did all they could to save me. They found my name and address sewn into the back of my shirt and the police informed my parents. On hearing of my condition my mother fainted. My father, ever the zealot, informed the church and the parish priest, Father Kennedy, drove to the hospital and administered the last rites over my semi-conscious body.

Twenty-four hours later I awoke with the hospital ward bathed in summer sunshine. Days passed in a blur as I made slow but sure progress towards recovery. At the end of my second week in hospital I received a letter from my mother full of loving concern and enclosing a silver chain with a medal of Saint Jude, the patron saint of hopeless cases, which she asked me to wear. My grandmother then made a surprise visit. She hugged me and we both wept a little. She had brought me some jam sandwiches and a small packet of digestive biscuits. My Aunt Mary Ann, her sister, had also given me a present of a bar of Cadbury's chocolate which she had been given by one of the airmen at the NAAFI where she worked. We were still in the depths of the war that had blistered its way across the whole of Europe, so food was scarce and luxuries almost impossible to come by.

My Nanna, for that was the particular name I called my grandmother at times of special intimacy, had two items of good news to tell me. The first was that my father, although he was in a reserve occupation, had been called up to serve in the Fleet Air Arm, the aircraft section of the Royal Navy, and was to leave immediately. The second was that it had been decided, between herself and my mother, that when I left hospital I should go to live with her until it was 'all got over'. Both these news items delighted me and released me from the fear of what would happen to me when I returned home. Too soon my Nanna had to leave and, since she had to travel on three different buses to get home to Blaydon-on-Tyne, I was overwhelmed by realizing the effort she had made to visit me. From my grandmother I learned the power of love and compassion; from my father I learned the potency of hate and bigotry.

Life in hospital continued to improve with the arrival of a parcel from my mother and grandmother. It contained a rice cake, which I later shared with the other boys on the ward, and a new pair of pyjamas plus a red, rough cotton dressing gown. Now I could move around the hospital without having to wear an institutional white gown. I could play with some of the other children who were at the recovery stage like me. I knew that my grandmother regularly bought clothing from an Indian man, a Sikh, who travelled around the streets with a huge suitcase containing items for sale.

Before I left hospital the medical staff removed my tonsils as a remedial measure. After the operation I awoke with a burning thirst that no amount of water could assuage. I longed for a drink of sparkling lemonade which my grandmother always kept in stone bottles, cooling in the pantry. I thought cold, fizzy lemonade was the most desirable, thirst-quenching drink ever, particularly on hot summer days or when you had just had your tonsils out. But for the moment I had to be content with cold tap water

At night I sometimes met up with Monty again in my dreams and relived happy moments of our time spent together. However, on awakening the reality of his death would cause me to weep into my pillow. I worried about how he must have felt at being taken away from me. When he became aware of what was happening to him, did he blame me for abandoning him? I agonized over how he must have felt and pined for him anew. After a time I was able to reconcile my thoughts about the event by the realization that bad things happen to good and innocent people and animals, too. I started to mature a little and I grew stronger, especially psychologically. I sensed that I would have to exercise great caution about openly revealing my affection for any animal pet whenever my father was around – if and when he ever came back from the Navy, which I hoped would never happen.

During those weeks in hospital I started to think about the chain of events in the first eight years of my life that had made me who I was – a troubled young boy who just couldn't seem to stop being at odds with the life around him.

BACK TO THE BEGINNING

It was my mother that I loved the most of my parents. Once my sisters arrived on the scene she had less time for me. The disadvantages of this was that I found it increasingly difficult to get her attention since the girls were very clingy, a characteristic which they bore even into adulthood. But I did have some exceptionally happy memories of the early times in my life when I could be alone with my mother. I recall many times before the age of five when my mother would sing to me when I was ill or just unable to get to sleep. She sang many different lullabies and melodies but the one I remember most cogently was the hymn 'I'll sing a hymn to Mary'. Strange are the ways of the mind, I realize, because whenever I am alone and feel out of sorts or sick, I can quite involuntarily hear in my head the sweet voice of my mother singing that hymn. After my sisters were born, I may have lost some of her attention but there were advantages too. While my mother was kept so busy attending to the demands of the girls, I had the freedom to spend time on my own and to wander freely. Once I learned the value of independence and freedom to roam I was in my element.

When my eldest sister Brenda was born it was late summer and my mother would take her in her pram, with me at her side, to places of serene natural beauty. We would go to the fields by the River Tyne where there was a small park and at other times we found a place in Blaydon Cemetery to sit and enjoy the tranquillity amongst the mature trees and flower beds adjacent to the weathered grave stones. Having become familiar with these places on walks in the company of my mother, I felt free to visit them on my own. Graveyards provide excellent sanctuaries for wildlife and it was this feature that drew me back there quietly to watch and study the birds that nested in the old trees. It was in such surroundings that I first caught a glimpse of a great spotted woodpecker hammering away with his beak working like a drill at an old oak tree. Song birds, thrushes, finches and blackbirds would nest there in abundance, along with many other birds that I could not at that stage identify. Several times I saw red squirrels and by careful observation found where one of them nested in a tree cavity. It was in the cemetery that I learned the skills necessary for observing wildlife, and also how to be stealthy in movement and clever at hiding. These skills were not only handy for studying wildlife: the Warden did not like little boys prowling around his graveyard so it was best to avoid him.

As a very young boy, my relationship with my mother might have been close, but, while lying in my hospital bed, I realized that the seeds of disharmony with my father had been present from the very beginning. When I was three, five years before Monty all too briefly brought joy to my life, our black cat,

Sooty, had two kittens, which I adored. After a few days my father gathered the tiny kittens up and led me into the backyard. He forced me to watch in great anguish as, with a stick of firewood, he held the little creatures down in a pail of water until they drowned. As I witnessed through my tears the little bubbles of air coming from the kittens' mouths I started to grasp that my father was satisfying something in himself by doing this. In later years I identified his cruelty to animals, as well as to myself and my mother, as gratifying a sense of power. The kittens and Monty were the victims but I was the real target of his vile actions. He held the reasons for his hatred close to his chest, and only once I became an adult would I truly understand the toxic effect that his secret had on my life.

It was a Friday in early May when at long last, having recovered from double pneumonia, I was discharged from hospital. My ever resourceful grandmother had enlisted the help of a friend, the headman in the delivery department of Blaydon Post Office where she worked as a cleaner, to collect me from Whickham hospital. So it was that shortly after eleven o'clock, when all postal deliveries in the area had been completed, a large red post office van arrived at the hospital entrance, delivered some mail, picked me up and conveyed me to my beloved Nanna's house by the railway lines. I sat among the parcels and bags of letters with a brown paper package wrapped in string containing my few belongings. It was like I was a special item of mail that had been misplaced but was now being delivered to the correct address.

My grandmother's house always exuded a special air of warmth. In most weathers there would be a coal fire lit, whatever the temperature, mainly to convey feelings of comfort and bonhomie but also as a means of drying the day's washing, which would often be hung over lengths of wood suspended from the ceiling by retractable cords. It was a happy home and it always gave me pleasure to be there. The house was decorated with antique furnishings that had been handed down through the family over many years. There was an old rocking chair of elaborately carved dark oak wood. It had cushioned arms and was among my favourite places to sit. The Victorian framed prints such as the *Monarch of the Glen*, the large hand-painted vases and the grey and blue chaise longue, which rested against the back wall of the sitting room, all served to give the house the ambience of an elegant bygone age.

Staying here, while recouping my health and spirits, was such a contrast to the spartan conditions under which I lived at home. My grandmother taught me how to make a cup of tea, how to fry an egg and the best way to make a rice pudding. She had time and patience for me and I thrived under her care. Best of all for an eager young mind, there was an extensive library of books that belonged to her brother, who was away working as a pastor for the Church Army. Uncle John was an educated man. He was also very generous to me and bought me toys. My father hated him and sometimes made my mother advertise 'Toys for sale' in the local paper in order to sell the toy cars, lead soldiers, a fort and a Meccano set my uncle had given me. This upset me greatly but there was nothing I could do about it.

All the great classics of literature adorned my Nanna's shelves: books by Dickens, Thackeray, George Eliot, the Brontës, Jane Austen, Hardy and Elizabeth Gaskell, as well as contemporary popular authors such as John Buchan and Catherine Cookson. I would never even have seen these books as a child if it wasn't for Uncle John's library. Faced with this multitude of literary treasures my mind raced with ecstasy and through long afternoons of reading I laid the basis for my future education. It was a priceless opportunity. Fortunately, my poor state of health enabled me to indulge a hunger for learning that my religious elementary schooling had not only failed to arouse but had discouraged as being dangerous and ungodly. Thus stimulated, my mind now awakened to new possibilities. I was learning how to think and, more importantly, how to think for myself without the gratuitous imposition of authoritative sanctions. I remember it as a special time in my life. That first night after getting out of hospital, lying in a big, luxurious bed with a lumpy mattress, I recalled the earlier times in my life when I had slept in this large, friendly old house under the care of my grandmother's love.

During the times that I spent living at my grandmother's house I often had occasion to visit her sister, my Aunt Mary

Ann, who was married to Joe, a miner. Uncle Joe had worked in the mines since he was twelve years old under primitive and harsh conditions. Many are the stories he told me of the back-breaking and dangerous working conditions that he and his fellow miners endured. One tragic story of the death of a miner in the 1920s sticks in my mind. The miner, a man who lived in the same row of pitman's cottages as Uncle Joe, had died in an underground rockfall. He was brought to the surface and his body placed on a cart. There were no ambulances or paramedics available in those days so one of the workmates of the dead man volunteered to take his body back to the pitman's cottage and inform his wife. The body was placed on a cart and covered with a tarpaulin, while the men returned to work. When the shift ended, at about 3 a.m., the workmate and my Uncle Joe wheeled the body to the dead man's home. Hammering on the door, he awakened the man's wife who opened the upstairs window and looked out. The friend of the dead man was embarrassed and, lacking any social graces, simply did not know how to tell her the tragic news. In the end he blurted out to her, 'Hey, guess who's died!'

My uncle would laugh at the black humour of this situation when he was relating the story, and remark that it was just part and parcel of the uncaring attitude caused by the hard conditions in which pitmen lived. Following a death, no compensation was available from the mine-owners except the man's unpaid wages up to the time of his death; his widow and family would have to vacate the cottage, which was owned by the mining company. 'Those are the conditions under which we worked, my lad, and not much has changed,' my Uncle Joe told me. 'So you take a mind of that and study hard at school to make something of yourself and stay clear of the mines.'

Often when I was playing in the street I would see Uncle Joe sitting on his stool on the pavement and smoking his clay pipe, especially if it was a sunny day. When I asked him why he was always sitting outside, he told me that miners liked to take every opportunity to sit out in the fresh air. At work they were chiefly surrounded by darkness, kneeling down in the narrow mine shafts to hew the coal with a pick axe. There were no washing or shower facilities at the mine so sometimes when I went to his house I would be confronted by the sight of Uncle Joe sitting in a tin bath in the kitchen with nothing on but the cap on his head and his pipe in his mouth. Aunt Mary Ann would be pouring kettles full of hot water around him to heat his bath. On seeing me he would call out for someone to fetch his clean trousers from which he would extract a sixpence to give to me. He was a kindly man who stooped as he walked, which was testimony to having spent years working crouched underground at the coalface in the mine tunnel. His eyes were always bright and smiling but the rims were forever marred by a black lining of coal dust. On Saturday nights he regularly went to the Miners' Arms Public House and got drunk. He died at the age of fifty-two from pneumonia and congestion of the lungs, a condition which in those days was called 'Miner's Lung'.

Gone and forgotten are many of the days of my early childhood but with some there is no forgetting. One such potent memory I can recall from the winter of early 1940, when I had just returned from London where I had been sent to stay whilst my mother gave birth to my sister Brenda. I was just five years old at the time. I was living with my grandmother at her big old house in the middle of Blaydon-on-Tyne because my father said it was best since my mother had the baby to care for and was too busy to look after me as well as the baby. I suspected it was really for his own convenience because he just didn't like having me around. It was still dark outside when my grandmother roused me from a deep warm sleep. When I got up the bedroom felt cold. It was January and outside icy frosts abounded. After leaving the cosy old bed covered by the heavy patchwork counterpane and slipping out of my pyjamas, I hurried to dress in the dim light from the half-open door leading to the main room.

'Come and get your porridge whilst it's still hot,' my grand-mother called.

After quickly rinsing my hands and face from the cold water tap in the small kitchen I hoisted myself on to a dining chair and sat up at the long table that was set for breakfast. My mother, who had come from home to join us having left my baby sister Brenda in the care of a neighbour, looked across at me with an affectionate good-morning smile. I yawned and rubbed my eyes under the harsh glare of the gaslight. Together we ate our porridge mixed with honey and drank strong tea as we quietly listened to the voice on the wireless announcing yet more tragic news. Our country was fighting against Adolf Hitler's German Army in the Second World War and the war was not going well for our troops.

Soon it was time to get going and, whilst my grandmother cleared the table and washed the dishes, my mother wound around my neck a thick woollen scarf which was knotted and hung down over my overcoat. She insisted I wore a cap that I hated, but she persisted. This was going to be a special day although I wasn't sure what it was all about. I expected that it was going to have something to do with the war: everything did, from the air-raid shelters, the lack of street lights and the taped up windows with their coverings of thick black cloth to having to be careful about picking up strange-looking things that might be a bomb.

At first it had been exciting seeing the news reels at the cinema showing fighter planes like the Spitfire and the Hurricane duelling with enemy planes. Then there were scenes of bombs dropping and soldiers fighting in foreign places. But when the war came nearer and started happening to us at home it was frightening. At anytime the air-raid sirens might start blaring and everybody quickly had to go down into the shelters in case the German aircraft dropped a bomb on our street. It was cold and damp in the shelters, and it was dark except for some lighted candles and small torches that some people brought with them. Not far from our street there was an anti-aircraft gun battery with huge searchlights pointing at the sky. It was there to defend the armament factories and the shipyards along the River Tyne from enemy bombers. One night during an air-raid, the guns exploded into life and started firing – all the windows in the street rattled as if they would break. Some people in the shelter cried out with fright, which made me feel scared as well.

It was still early in the morning when I left the house with my mother and grandmother. The sky was just beginning to grow light. It was cold with white hoarfrost covering the roofs and the pavements, and I stuck my hands in the pockets of my coat to keep warm.

'Where are we going?' I asked my mother.

'You'll see soon enough,' was all the reply I received.

Still curious, I asked my grandmother the same question.

'We're going to the railway station to see the soldiers off.' This answer did nothing to allay my anxiety.

'But where are the soldiers going?' I persisted.

'They're going across the sea to France to fight the German Army,' my grandmother answered.

I had more questions to ask but just then we were joined by a lot of other women, some with children and babies, all walking in the same direction. My mother and grandmother were soon caught up in earnest conversation with their friends. As we drew near to the railway station we became part of a large crowd queuing to go inside. At another entrance, which was sealed off from the public, there were lots of soldiers and more of them kept arriving in huge Army trucks. They all had a grim, fierce appearance. They were wearing steel helmets and had equipment strapped to their belts and across their backs. They all carried rifles. A young soldier, with two white stripes on his uniform, was unloading green boxes from the back of a lorry. When he glanced my way, he winked and gave me a broad smile. Not knowing what to do, I looked away shyly.

At long last the queue surged forward and we moved out of the icy January wind blowing down the street into the shelter of the station. Inside there was a crush of people struggling to find a place to view the departure of the Army. In front of us, an old man with a walking stick lost his balance, fell to the ground and had to be helped back on to his feet. He had grey whiskers on his chin just like my Uncle Joe, the coal miner. The old man was wearing some medals across his chest, which my grandmother told me were for his service in the First World War.

Everybody was trying to get to the front of the barriers the police had put on the platforms. The soldiers were now lining up on the other side of the barriers awaiting the arrival of the trains. We were pushed about and I held on tight to my grandmother's hand as the crowd shoved their way around us. We got jammed into a corner and I lost my cap but I didn't say anything. Then by a stroke of luck, when a group in front of us burst forward, we found ourselves on the bridge that spanned the railtracks and joined the two platforms. I was forced up against the railings of the bridge in front of my mother and Nanna. I felt a little bit crushed but I now had an excellent view of everything that was happening.

By this stage both platforms were packed with soldiers milling around, smoking, waving and sometimes calling across to someone they knew in the crowd. I gripped the cold iron railings so that I wouldn't lose my place at the front and kept turning round to make sure my grandmother and mother were still close behind me. I passed the time by watching people's breath making small clouds of steam in the freezing air and kept stamping my feet to keep warm. It wasn't long before there was a tremendous rumbling. The earth shook and the bridge trembled in protest at the roaring blast of a monstrous steam-powered railway engine as it thundered into view. It belched clouds of steam and groaned and hissed its way into the station like a giant living thing. Then a hush descended over the crowd of public onlookers and soldiers alike. Next, there came the sound of many carriage doors slamming as the soldiers began to embark. Somewhere in the midst of all the noise a baby could be heard crying but no matter how I craned my neck to see where, it was impossible to tell in that vast multitude of people.

As the hush of expectancy was broken there was a feverish onset of talking again within the assembled crowd. Some people on the platforms started shouting messages to loved ones they thought they might never see again and the station was filled with an anguish that was tangible: the air itself seemed to vibrate with emotions of imminent separation and desperation at the going of the soldiers. Tension wracked the atmosphere of the station and impassioned the crowd. Then, at the far end of one of the platforms, a tall, importantly dressed soldier carrying a long stick began shouting orders to the remaining soldiers who, at his command, began hurrying to get on to the train. One soldier was suddenly singled out for everyone's attention. He was the young happy looking soldier who had winked at me outside the station. He was standing apart from the others who were scrambling to get on to the train. I could see him talking to some of the officers who nodded at him and then I knew that something special was about to happen.

Suddenly he drew himself up, standing alone on the platform, and in a clear tenor voice that carried all over the station he began to sing. At the sound of his voice all the other sounds slowly stopped and all talking was hushed as people just listened to his voice. A palpable wave of emotion swept through the assembled throng. Then as the familiar tunes he sang were recognized the waiting crowd gradually began to join in and sing along with him. The songs they sang seemed to be cheerful and yet had a deep and pervading sadness about them as mothers, wives and children became aware through the words of the tunes what it would be like to lose a loved one in this hateful war. 'Good bye Dolly I must leave you, though it breaks my heart to go . . .'

Soon everybody was joining in. When I looked up I saw that my mother and grandmother were both singing and crying at the same time, as were many of the other women I could see. At the sight of their tears I was overwhelmed and began to cry, too.

Finally, all the soldiers had boarded the train. Some of them leant out of the carriage windows, still singing, whilst the train, in contrast to its noisy arrival, started to pull away almost silently as if in deference to the heartache of the charged situation. Abruptly, as if the sentiments could not be left unspoken, the tune they sang changed to the words of a familiar song that I often heard on the wireless. It rang out loudly through the station in a defiant as well as hopeful tone: 'We'll meet again, don't know where, don't know when, but I know we'll meet again some sunny day . . .'

As the train gathered momentum and finally disappeared into the grey light of a bleak winter's day the singing gradually petered out. Handkerchiefs that had been used to wave goodbye were now pressed into service to wipe away tears as the crowd slowly and quietly left the station in a kind of reverential calm. Gone was the excited babble of the last two hours to be replaced by looks of grim-faced reality as, alone with their thoughts, everyone made their way home. Many would be returning to a house that wouldn't be the same until the man of the house, whether father, husband or son, returned home, safe and sound.

Meanwhile the horrors of war continued to assail my little boy's mind. At school lessons were constantly interrupted by air raids of German bombers which pummelled the areas around our small town with high explosive bombs that kept us awake at night and frightened us with scenes of devastation in the morning. One night in 1940, when my mother was staying with us at my grandmother's house, the warning siren had hardly sounded when a terrific bomb blast shook the house and caused the ceiling in my bedroom to collapse on top of me. The plaster covered me completely and my mother had to pull me out by the feet. She hurriedly brushed away the plaster from my face and pyjamas. I was coughing and spluttering because some of the dust had got into my mouth and up my nose, but my mother yelled at me in great urgency to get downstairs and into the bomb shelter whilst she carried the baby and blankets to keep us warm. On the wireless the Prime Minister Winston Churchill called it 'our darkest hour'.

Later in June, near my sixth birthday, we learned of the tragedy of Dunkirk, when after suffering a heavy defeat what remained of our Army had to be evacuated by ship and virtually any kind of seaworthy boat the military could obtain. The soldiers were standing on the shore or in the shallow water like sitting ducks, waiting to be rescued whilst subjected to heavy enemy artillery fire and strafing from German fighter planes. In the days that followed my grandmother was kept busy in her spare time consoling the many young wives living in the streets around us who had received the dreaded telegram from the War Office telling them that their husbands or sons had been killed or were missing. My grandmother remarked to me, 'There'll be no cheerful songs for the singing now.'

It was a very harrowing, sad time to then see the many men in uniform wearing bandages covering their wounds as they hobbled, grim-faced, around our streets suffering the fear that they would soon be back fighting the war. They were the lucky ones who got rescued from the beach. Many didn't, my grandmother said. It made me think of the young soldier who had winked at me on the day the soldiers had left and who had led the singing in the station. I hoped he had survived but I never got to know. If he was still alive, I doubt that he was still singing to the crowds. Everyone knew that we would need more than songs and a brief show of emotional fortitude now. Our Army had taken a severe beating and there was the imminent threat of a German invasion of our country. People were afraid and spoke about it constantly. The talk on the wireless was all about how we should be ready to fight but I was just a young child, already scared by what I had seen of the war on the newsreels. I was very frightened but I didn't dare to say anything because I knew that all the grown-ups around me – family, teachers and neighbours – were dreadfully fearful too.

All civilians, even children, were soon supplied with gas masks in case the German planes dropped bombs filled with poisonous gas. I hated to wear mine and adults, even family, looked hideously frightening with their faces covered by the masks. It was a very worrying time for everybody but it was an enormous relief to me to be free from my father's presence. There was a different mood in our home and the dread I always felt when he was at home was thankfully missing. I continued to hope that he would never ever return, but of course he eventually did.

Our community suffered deaths and destruction of property during the early years of the war and many families we knew lost loved ones, but there was still an air of defiance abroad amongst the local population. People were prepared to accept all manner of privation and still make the most of it. Once when the local grapevine spread the news that supplies of fresh fruit had reached shops in the town, my grandmother sent me to queue at a shop selling bananas while she queued at another shop where oranges were for sale. After queuing for two hours I was given a ration of two bananas. On the way back to my grandmother's house I met up with a crowd of people who could not get any further down the road because a huge swarm of bees had infested the walls of the lane and they were buzzing angrily. I had to backtrack around two streets to return home. Later it was learned that some criminals, probably black marketeers – the men and women who acquired food illicitly and sold it at inflated prices – had raided a local man's beehives for honey and destroyed them in the process, forcing the bees to take flight with the queen and look for a new home. Several people got stung and there was an awful hullabaloo. My grandmother returned from her shopping trip with two oranges, which together with the bananas was the first fruit we had seen for nearly two years.

Early in 1943, while my father was still away with the Fleet Air Arm, there were signs that the war was beginning to turn in the Allies' favour. Late one night the sirens started screaming as usual. As the German bombers were making their approach to the north-east coast to bomb munitions factory targets along the River Tyne, a fighter squadron of seventeen Spitfires were scrambled from Acklington Airfield to engage them in combat. My Uncle John, who was an air raid warden at the time, came to the shelter and took me up on the iron bridge over the railway track to see what was happening in the sky. There were several other people already on the bridge watching the scene taking place in the air. It was a moonlit night and from the bridge we had a clear view of a fighter plane attacking a German bomber. My uncle said the enemy plane was a Dornier which would use flares to illuminate the route to guide the bombers to their target. As we watched it was shot down and crashed not far from the bridge over the Tyne at Scotswood. The small group of onlookers on our bridge broke into shouts of 'hurrah' at this and applauded with much clapping of their hands. Later, I learned that several more enemy planes were destroyed by the Spitfire squadron that night.

I felt really excited by seeing the Dornier shot down, and next day at school I drew a picture of the aerial skirmish in art class, but my schoolfriends said that I had made up the story.

When we got back to the house my grandmother reprimanded Uncle John for putting us both in danger but he said that he thought it would be good for me to see how we were beginning to win the war. As indeed we were. The news on the wireless was much more positive from our point of view and there was a lot of talk in the street and around the town that before too long the Allies would be invading Europe to finish off Hitler and the Nazis. Most people thought that the war would soon be over and these sentiments even percolated down to the children's games we played in the streets. We pretended to be commandos invading German-occupied Europe and we lay in ambush to shoot at anyone who passed. This game-playing escalated one night into a real fight with some boys from another street and we all suffered bruises and bloody noses. I also had a rip in my pullover but my grandmother sewed it up before my mother could become aware of it.

The sad thing was that although the Allies looked like they had turned the corner, many young soldiers and innocent civilians were still being killed every single day. My Uncle John, a religious man whose idea of how to be a good Christian was much more broad-minded than my father's, said that we should pray for everybody including the Germans, who were dying through no fault of their own. Rather than just being filled with hatred for the enemy, people started to agree that the war had been a terrible thing for both sides.

We were expecting to hear about victory and the end of the war any day but the first time I realized it was over was when

I heard a commotion in the street and saw an impromptu parade of young children marching up the lane. They were led by an older boy called Richard who suffered from Down's syndrome and who was cruelly referred to by the street children as 'Daft Dick'. As he marched along, he proudly had a broomstick over his shoulder in imitation of a rifle. My grandmother put the wireless on and immediately we heard the crowds cheering in London's Parliament Square and the announcer saying that the war was over, Germany had surrendered, Adolf Hitler was dead and the Allies were victorious. There was a feeling of utter relief that was visceral. For some time it was hard to believe that it was all over. And, of course, I began to fear the return of my father who was being demobilized earlier than expected. His Air Craft Carrier Squadron had been assigned to join the American Fleet in the war against Japan, but Japan had then surrendered so he was on his way home.

SOJOURN FROM TROUBLE

During those years just before the war I was not wanted at home. Most of the time I was able to stay with my grandmother but when I was nearly four years old my mother had become pregnant with Brenda and it was felt that my grandmother would be needed to look after her for a while when the baby came. So I was shipped off to stay in London at the home of my Uncle Fred and Aunt Betty, my mother's cousin, who lived in Bromley, Kent, on the outskirts of the city. Of course, I felt rejected by this turn of events – even if my parents did not seem to want me, at least I had always had the comfort of staying with my grandmother. However, my stay in Bromley turned out to be one of the happiest periods of my childhood.

I found for the first time in my life that I was surrounded by people who enjoyed being together and welcomed me into the midst of their happiness with open arms. I felt that I now really belonged to a loving, happy family. It felt so good and I was living what seemed to a carefree life – which for me was something of a novel sensation. I woke up every morning with happy thoughts and looked forward to the day without fear of doing something wrong – there was only the anticipation of enjoyable times ahead. All this was in complete contrast to my last morning at home before Uncle Fred came to collect me for the long trip to London.

My mother was having a very sickly time with her pregnancy and I was worried about her but my father seemed to resent my presence and had no doubt been the prime mover in sending me away. He came home for his lunch and he called me to him to show me the reddest, most desirable apple I had ever seen. Holding it in front of me, he snarled that the apple was for my mother alone and he threatened me with all kinds of violence if I touched it. He then placed it away in a moveable cupboard we called a press. My father's words hurt me deeply because I loved my mother and would have given her everything I had to please her. I certainly would never have stolen her apple.

My cousin June, my Aunt Betty and Uncle Fred's daughter, was exactly my age having been born on the very same day as myself. We were like twins and were playmates from the very beginning. Freda, her sister, was much younger and couldn't keep up with us, but she liked it when we all played ball games in the big garden of the house. In their family I was given a sense of self-esteem that was previously unknown to me. I was often indulged in ways I had never really known, especially by my Aunt Betty's mother, Aunt Meggie, who reminded me of my grandmother. Not surprisingly, I never felt homesick.

During my stay with them the family had arranged to go on a summer holiday to Clacton-on-Sea and it thrilled me to know that I was to go with them. It was the first holiday I had ever experienced. The holiday at Clacton had many significant episodes for me that brought out my love for nature. It was my first contact with the sea. For me, like many children, splashing about in warm waters at the seaside was a wonderful encounter with nature, releasing my pent-up feelings and stripping away my inhibitions. I splashed about with abandon in the warm water and discovered a new aspect to nature to enjoy and revere. On some days we would all go to the outdoor swimming pool and it was there, with the help of my cousins, that I finally learned to swim.

One day my excitement reached a crescendo when I discovered tiny, eel-like fish swimming around my legs as I splashed deeper into the waves and realized that the sea really was inhabited with all sorts of living things. It was quite a revelation. It filled me with a sense of awe about the sea, which has never left me. At night, in our holiday chalet, I listened with wonder to the sound of the sea. I slept a deep sleep of contentment while lulled by the swish of the tide as the waves whispered and then slapped against the shore.

Back at the house in Bromley there were many further opportunities to excite my burgeoning interest in natural things. It was decided that I could go and sleep at my Aunt Meggie's house, only two doors away from the family, where I could have a bedroom to myself rather than sleeping in the same bedroom as June and her younger sister, Freda. Next to my Aunt Meggie's house lived a bachelor who bred white pedigree rabbits. Observing my interest in his rabbits from across the back garden fence, he invited me over to meet his pedigree creatures. I was enthralled to become acquainted with these soft-furred animals that were the main focus of his life. We became friends and he offered to give me one of his prize breeds for free, which normally would have fetched a sizeable sum of money. Unfortunately, I knew that I had to turn down his kind offer as I was all too aware that my father appeared to hate wildlife of any sort. I was afraid of his reaction to a pet rabbit and knew that the joy of bringing one home would only end in terrible unhappiness. I contented myself with helping the neighbour to care for his animals, feeding them and playing with them on the lawn. I soon began to share his fascination for them.

My carefree time came to an end when I was told that my return home was imminent. I cried when I left because I was being torn away from the embrace of a truly loving family, unlike my own back at Blaydon-upon-Tyne. As usual, my father didn't seem too pleased to have his son back at home, and on the day I returned he warned me in no uncertain terms that I was not to go anywhere near my newborn sister, Brenda. In fact, although I heard her crying at night sometimes, I was not allowed to even set eyes upon her until six weeks later when one day my mother was feeding her and motioned me over to behold the baby. She was pink-fleshed and blue-eyed and I immediately began to feel jealous. Subsequently this state of affairs escalated as I witnessed the amount of attention that was lavished on my sister, especially by my father, as well as the multitude of baby toys that were bought for her amusement.

At Christmas I became increasingly aware of just how far I was being marginalized – I just didn't seem to be a proper part of the family. In previous Christmases, no one except my grandmother and my Uncle John had bothered to buy me presents of any worth to me at Christmas time. I would receive some new clothes, and occasionally a snakes-and-ladders board game or a small bar of chocolate would be thrown in. Now, in the run up to Christmas, I observed the family's efforts to provide my baby sister with a plethora of cuddly toys, dolls and delicious things to eat. I began to think that times had changed and so I put in a request for a model fire engine, for which I longed.

Christmas Eve arrived and in a frenzy of trepidation I awaited the morning only to find that I had yet another snakes-and-ladders board game, an orange and an apple in my stocking. I should have known better, but I was filled with an all-consuming disappointment. Even my grandmother and Uncle John had only bought me packets of sweets that I didn't really like such as liquorish and boiled bull's eyes. In contrast, my sister Brenda received an abundance of baby toys and even a doll's pram which seemed like madness because she couldn't even walk at this stage. I consoled myself by disappearing and spending the day in Winlaton Woods watching birds and crested newts by a small stream deep in the woods. I was missed when I didn't turn up for lunch but my father thought that it was best to just forget about me.

My grandmother called in at home to see the baby and when she heard that I was missing, she grew concerned. She went to Billy Murphy's house and asked him to find me. Billy was my best friend at school. We sat together in class and were often caned for talking together or giving the wrong answers to questions in mental arithmetic sessions. I helped Billy with his schoolwork and he helped me fight off bullies in the school playground. At weekends we played around the streets together. He knew the places in the woods that I favoured and often joined me there. True to form, Billy caught up with me and we both went back to my grandmother's house and ate freshly cooked sausage rolls and a dish each of homemade rice pudding.

As I think back to earlier times I recall that my parents seemed to be quite happy to farm me out to relatives and neighbours as often as they could. They never seemed to want to take me anywhere with them, which meant that I spent a lot of my life, from the age of two onwards, with a variety of strange characters – mostly local old women – who treated me with extreme kindness for which I am eternally grateful. Meanwhile, my parents went dancing or to the cinema, while at weekends they invariably joined the betting fraternity at Scotswood Greyhound Racing Stadium.

These older ladies included the aged aunt of my mother, Aunt Hannah, with whom I regularly spent nights at weekends. She would often entertain her neighbours who were of a similar age and they taught me to play card games such as whist and snap, as well as dominoes and draughts. We seemed to spend hours playing these games and betting on the outcomes with a pile of halfpennies as stake money. At times I cheated as I got carried away by the fun of the games, but no one seemed to mind – just playing the game and filling in the time was what mattered most. Thinking back to those times I now realize how privileged I was to share the company of these dear old ladies who were in effect surrogate aunts. They rarely became impatient with me and they were always caring and loving, which boosted my lack of confidence. I always felt much favoured by them. They also fed me delicious ham sandwiches and homemade chips.

The ladies often took the time to talk with me and related stories about their lives that stimulated my young mind. I learnt about the world through their eyes and I was able to tap into their wealth of experience to understand more about life. The contrast with my home life was marked: in the evenings when we were all at home together my parents rarely spoke to me, being too busy with their own concerns. If I agitated them by asking questions I would usually be told to 'go and play with something'. The gentle old ladies never treated me in this way. We tended to laugh a lot of the time and they seemed to enjoy my company. The wireless was always on: 'Just in case,' my Aunt Hannah would say, 'we get invaded by the Hun.' Some of the other ladies said they would rather not know. I tried not to think about it because we had no guns or swords with which to protect ourselves from the German invaders, even though the Prime Minister, Winston Churchill, kept saying that we would fight them on the beaches and in the backstreets. I decided that if they did come I would hide somewhere with my grandmother until the Germans were beaten and gone.

At this time my grandmother figured large in my life. I would usually stay with her at weekends and we would go what she called 'visiting'. And so I often found myself in strange houses with strange people – and some of them really were rather peculiar. My grandmother always dressed elegantly on these occasions and had a hat adorned with several exotic bird feathers that she especially favoured. One such visit turned out to be very unusual indeed and it stimulated my growing interest in wildlife, but in a very unorthodox manner.

My grandmother had a friend called Hannah Doby, an ex-teacher who held very eccentric views about life. She lived in an eighteenth-century cottage near the Dene, a kind of public park. Her cottage was cosy and warm as well as being well-furnished and remarkably clean in spite of what I was to witness there when I visited with my grandmother. We were offered honeyed tea, hot buttered scones with homemade strawberry jam and rice cake that she had made herself, all of which was delicious. During our tea my attention was drawn to a large cage by the window. It contained two birds that whistled musically and looked to be well cared for and contented. Miss Doby noticed my interest in her birds and she introduced me to them, calling them by their names, Sugar and Spice. They were beautiful, yellow canaries – a little touch of summer sunlight in the window. They were obviously very fond of her and both of them came close to the cage when she called them to receive, each in turn, a morsel of rice cake.

I was fascinated with them so she said, as a treat for being such a good boy and showing interest in her birds, she would allow me to see her other 'wild pets'. Not knowing what to expect I simply stayed by the window next to the canaries. Beckoning me to join her from across the room near the fire she drew her stool close to the stone fireplace and began to whistle softly, interspersing the whistling with softly murmured words of endearment. I wasn't sure what would happen and cast a glance back at my grandmother who was calmly watching us whilst eating a scone and holding a cup of tea in her hand. Suddenly there was a wild scrambling by the hearth in front of the coal fire and, to my astonishment, a pair of grey mice appeared. They sat up and begged in front of Miss Doby like two miniature dogs. Behind me I heard a coughing and spluttering as my Nanna choked on her tea at the sight. To me it was like a scene from my Mickey Mouse comic come alive.

Miss Doby leaned forward and, addressing the mice by name – Chico and Choo – she introduced them to me as she fed them pieces of cake. When she had finished feeding them she stroked each of the mice with her fingers and bade them goodbye.

She then turned to me and said, 'Well, what do you think of that, boy?'

'Wonderful,' I replied with childlike enchantment.

'These mice are my friends,' she continued. 'They are part of nature's plan to live in tune with other life and with humans and we do not have the right to hurt or kill them just because we are too selfish to share what we have.'

We left Hannah Doby's cottage shortly after the performance with the mice and once outside my grandmother said that she wouldn't be going back there again. She told me that rodents, particularly mice, were dirty creatures and carried disease, and she wished that she hadn't eaten anything in case the mice had been at it. But my little boy's eyes had seen that after eating the offerings of rice cake each mouse had proceeded to lick its paws and wash its face. In contrast, some of the boys I played with around the backstreets always seemed to have dirty faces, with grime, chocolate and the remnants of cake smeared around their lips and chins. Perhaps they could do with a lesson from the mice.

In bed later that night I recalled what I had seen and I was impressed by the words of the strange old lady who appeared to be gentle and loving as well as wise. She made me think more about nature and what it meant in my life. How could I fit into nature's plan with all the other wild creatures? I went to sleep with no idea how I might accomplish this, but once again, I felt that studying nature was somehow going to be of vital importance to my life.

One day, at the age of six going on seven, I was playing in the backstreet with an old tennis ball during a half-term school holiday. I was throwing the ball against the wall and trying to catch it when it bounced back, which was good catching practice because the back lane was laid with cobbles and the ball tended to swerve unexpectedly when it bounced. Across from where I was playing that morning a backyard door opened and a man came out carrying his bin for the refuse collection. On seeing me he stopped, stared at me a while and then gestured for me to approach him. He pointed into his backyard where there was a collection of balls of all shapes and sizes.

'You can have all of those if you want,' he said in a gravelly voice. 'They came over my wall and I wouldn't throw them back because they are a nuisance to me but you can have them if you like.'

I ran forward and scooped up three or four of the best-looking ones and turned to say thank you.

'You're welcome, sonny,' he said. 'But don't throw them back over my wall.'

I scurried away with my collection of balls and stored them in a box in our backyard under a lean-to roof.

'Where did you get those?' my mother said from the open back door.

I explained and told her that I did say thank you before she could ask.

'That would be Mr Markham. Why don't you ask him if he needs any errands done? He might pay you, you never know.'

And that is how I came to be acquainted with our neighbour, Mr H. Markham. I had seen the 'H' on some of the used envelopes he threw out in his rubbish bin. I never found out what it stood for but decided that it was probably 'Henry' simply because I had heard about a king called Henry at school. He took up my offer to run messages for him and would pay me in pennies when I had finished. Much more important from my point of view was that he engaged me in conversation. At first it was simply the sort of polite talk about day-to-day concerns but when he realized that I was interested in talking with him, and that I was enthusiastic about wildlife and learning about nature, then our conversations took a more serious turn.

He started to tell me about all the animals that he had kept and cared for, and how earlier in his life he had studied Biology and had attended lectures by the eminent biologist Sir Julian Huxley – the brother of Aldous Huxley, author of *Brave New World*. He told me that Julian Huxley thought that human beings had been developing as a species for many millions of years through the process of evolution. In fact, it had taken three billion years for humankind to arrive at the stage it had reached now. Mr Markham said that Professor Huxley explained that through this long period of development humankind alone had developed what he called 'consciousness of self and all the possibilities this brings to us'.

'When Roo, my cat, looks in the mirror,' explained Mr Markham, 'he thinks he sees another cat but when we look in a mirror we know that we are looking at ourselves. This is because our human minds have evolved to the point that we are aware not just of ourselves but of other people and the world in a way that gives us the power to change things through what we think and imagine. This makes us responsible for what happens in life because we can do something about it.'

He asked me if I understood what he said and I told him that I thought it meant we could do things to help nature since we could see what needed to be done but a bird or a rabbit couldn't do that.

'Good boy!' he said.

Later in my life I came to the same conclusions as Mr Huxley and Mr Markham.

On many days, after I'd run his errands, he would take time to describe some of his experiences with animals whilst he lived and worked in foreign countries like Egypt and Morocco. Recognizing my appetite for knowledge about the natural world he astounded my mind with stories of exploring the Amazon forest and hunting for unknown kinds of orchids and other plants. One of the tales he told me was about a ferocious man-eating jaguar that stalked his party in the deep jungle and attacked one of his native bearers one night when they were camped near the river. He told me that they tried to escape from the big cat by travelling downriver by raft and canoe, but the creature followed their progress from the riverbanks. The party was filled with fear as the huge yellow beast, with its black spots and markings, moved stealthily along the bank and affixed them with its fierce stare from the jungle shadows.

'Why didn't you shoot it?' I asked him.

'We did not go there to kill but to explore and learn. The jaguar was only following the instincts of her nature as a wild inhabitant of her jungle world, she only killed for food; if we had killed her it would have been out of revenge, which is a petty human trait.'

'So you were the intruders into her land where she had the right to roam free,' I replied.

'Why, Denis O'Connor, my boy, you're a psychologist!' He said with an approving nod and benign smile.

'What's a psychologist? I asked him.

'A learned person who seeks to understand why animals and people do the things that they do.' Mr Markham didn't realize it, but he had just opened the door to my future profession in psychology.

His attention and approval started to boost my feeble self-esteem and fuelled my appetite for knowledge. I was beginning to look forward to the times when Mr Markham wasn't busy and had time to talk with me, which was usually on the weekends or school holidays. I learned through him that some people can talk to children in a way that puts them at ease and that these adults make the best teachers. He was helping me to learn about life and was feeding my awakening interest in all things natural. He let me look at his aquarium, which was full of exotic coloured fish. I never tired of watching the different types of fish, which would swim, flit or just stay almost perfectly motionless in the water. He also let me stroke Roo, his ginger tomcat. He said he called the cat 'Roo' because he 'rued' the day he'd allowed the cat to stay and 'take over his house'. In truth, he seemed to have a great deal of affection for Roo, a healthy looking cat who had his own cushion and feeding bowls, and appeared very comfortable and pleased with his lot.

One day before school I brought Mr Markham's newspaper and loaf of bread back from the local shop, but he didn't answer when I called to him at the half-open back door. Thinking he was perhaps busy with his aquarium, I pushed the door open and went inside. He was sitting on his wooden chair by the table, wearing the black beret he usually wore, but something was wrong about the way he appeared. He was staring ahead but not looking at anything. I called to him again but he just nodded his head and didn't respond to my urgent enquiries about his condition. Then suddenly he spoke.

'I'm cold, so cold!' he said.

He then just gently collapsed forward and laid his head on the kitchen table, which was covered in worn, flowered oil cloth.

I stood there in a sort of paralysis, not wanting to move, until Mrs Angus, his cleaning woman, breezed into the room.

She took everything in at a glance, immediately understanding what must have happened.

'Go and be about your business, lad,' she said to me and I ran to tell my mother.

I later learned that Mr Markham had suffered a kind of illness which my mother called a 'stroke' and had died shortly afterwards. His married sister came to claim the house and one day, when I saw furniture from the house being loaded into a cart, I went into the yard and asked a workman if he'd seen the cat. He told me that I'd better ask inside. Just then I was confronted by a large woman who demanded to know what I was doing.

'I'm looking for Roo, Mr Markham's cat.' I then explained to her how I had known Mr Markham.

'Well, boy,' she said in that haughty way that some adults use to address insignificant children, 'I do not want my brother's cat so if you like it then I suggest you take it otherwise I'll have it put away.' With that she stomped back into the house and disappeared, leaving me standing in the yard. Workmen kept pushing past me as they carried one item after another from the house out to the cart and kept telling me to 'Mind yourself' and 'Get out of the way.'

Deciding to be bold I sneaked into the house and began looking for Roo. Since the sofa had already disappeared along with the cat's cushion I couldn't think where to look for him. Suddenly I heard a screech as one of the furniture removers stood on Roo's paw. This was accompanied by a curse from the workman and a sorrowful looking Roo limped into sight.

'Come on pal,' I said. 'You're with me now!'

After a brief discussion my mother agreed to let me keep Roo but with the proviso that she didn't know what my father would say about it. She also added that she had no house-keeping money to spend on feeding a cat and so I quickly agreed that he would share my meals.

Later that week, one day when I was alone in the house and was busy reading my *Dandy* comic, there was a knock on the door and Mr Markham's sister stood there looking down at me.

'My brother's will has just been read and he left you £50,' she said. She then thrust an envelope containing pound notes into my hand and walked away.

My mother was out shopping so I decided to keep the money a secret until I had decided what to do with it and immediately hid it in amongst my comics in a cupboard upstairs in my room. The next time I went to the post office I would put the money in my savings account, which already held the grand total of seventeen shillings and sixpence – everything I had managed to save so far.

The following day when I came in from school my mother was waiting for me and beside her sat my father, wearing his 'Day of Judgement' face. Spread out on the table was the £50 which my mother had discovered when she was tidying my room.

'Where did you get this money from?' growled my father.

'It was from Mr Markham. He left it to me when he died.'

I didn't see the slap coming but I reeled and was knocked to the floor by the blow.

'You liar,' he shouted. 'You stole this money from that neighbour's house, didn't you? You took the money from where the old man kept it, didn't you?'

My father refused to listen to my protests and urgent explanations. Still dizzy and feeling sick from the smack, I was grabbed by the ear and marched into the backstreet where my father banged on Mr Markham's back door. Eventually the old man's sister opened the door in answer to my father's loud thumping. It clearly emerged in his conversation with her that I was telling the truth – not that he was placated in any way by that information.

'So you thought to keep it hidden from me, you greedy little sod, in spite of the fact of what it costs me to feed and care for you. Well, mister, that is the last you'll see of this money. It can go a part way towards your upkeep from now on.'

Luckily my mother hadn't told my father about Roo, so I sneaked him up to bed that night and in the semi-darkness told him all about the events. The big ginger tomcat liked a comfortable life and spent most of the daytime sleeping. He preferred to roam the streets and gardens at night but he was always there in the morning awaiting his breakfast. In the end, despite my best efforts to rehabilitate him, Roo would not stay with me. He was not partial to eating egg and chips nor did he relish homemade broth. It pained me to see him go but I was pleased to learn that he had decided to take up residence with a retired couple in a house not far from our own. I'm sure Mr Markham would have been pleased. I rarely saw Roo again but sometimes I caught sight of him high up on a backyard wall looking very superior. I do not think he thought much of me or my diet.

As for my £50, my mother saw little of it and the bookmakers no doubt profited the most from it. I respected and admired Mr Markham and it was generous of him to leave me some money. I still remember many of things he said to me. One of them was to save my pocket money and buy books because 'books are the keys to learning.' Another thing he told me was the only real sin in this world was when people made war on nature.

'Remember,' he said, 'if you destroy creatures, trees and plants then you destroy something in yourself. Humanity is as much a part of nature as the birds and the butterflies.' Later in my life his words found resonance for me in the words of the Indian philosopher Satish Kumar, who said that we are not life separate from nature, we are nature.

I took these words to heart and they remained a significant part of my thinking for the rest of my life. Mr Markham was a very wise man, far superior to my teachers at junior school who seemed obsessed with religion and rote learning. I hated school but I had a high opinion of Mr Markham, a dignified but unpretentious old man in a black French beret who took the time to talk to a curious boy. You can never tell who lives across from you and what surprises each day might bring.

A WILDCAT IN SCOTLAND

When I was growing up the relationship between my parents was fraught and there were many fractious rows, which often took place in my presence and caused me no end of stress.

On one occasion, when I was four-and-a-half years old, I saw them rowing on the upstairs landing when my father hit my mother with his fist. She fell back and tumbled down the stairs. On impulse I charged at him and started pummelling his legs and screaming. With an open-handed swipe he sent me flying down the stairs after my mother. I rolled down the whole flight of stairs, landing in my mother's lap as she sat stunned on the floor near the front door.

No further words were spoken but that evening, when my father was out working overtime, my mother packed a small suitcase with some of our clothes and took her 'running away money' from its hiding place in the back recess behind a drawer. We left on the night train to Inverness in Scotland. We were going to the home of my mother's aunt, sister to my mother's father, who lived in a big old house on the west coast. My mother had stayed there a few times as a girl and had been told she would be always welcome. We travelled fast and far during the night, but by morning we were still miles away from our destination. I was tired and hungry but there was no let up in our travels until a rickety old bus deposited us in a small village on the border of the Highlands.

We walked by the path along the sea shore until we came to a stalwart grey stone building that stood at the end of a row of houses facing the sea. We were exhausted. A knock at the heavy-looking wooden door brought a gaunt woman bustling to see her unexpected visitors. Once she recognized my mother her surprise turned to evident delight and we were welcomed into a warm home that smelled richly of homemade food. I was tired but desperately hungry and although Aunt Sheilis made a terrific fuss of me it was only when I had supped a bowl of hot highland broth that I was able to fully relax at journey's end. I looked across at the relieved face of my mother and wondered, as only a child can, what would happen to us now. But with the warming essences of my new found aunt's soup in me I snuggled into a corner of the long sofa and drifted into dreamland. The murmur of the adults' conversation and the warmth from the coal fire lulled me far away to a secure place in my mind where I could totally rejoice in being safe.

I awoke slowly as though emerging from a fog. Outside I could hear the wailing of what seemed to be a huge chorus of seagulls as they cried their hymn to the sea. The sea in turn seemed to sigh and commenced a rhythmic tempo as the waves pounded and crashed on the rocky shore of the bay. I was lost, far from home, in a foreign country, in a strange bed in a different house and I was sore all over from my fall down the stairs at home. Yet I felt strangely comforted as my head filled with the soothing primeval noise of the sea from outside the bedroom window.

Soon I could hear my mother's voice talking to someone nearby but I didn't move since I was more content just to lie quietly and listen to the gulls. I was happily reminded of the holiday in Clacton-on-Sea with my Uncle Fred, aunts and cousins, but this was much further away from home and I wondered if we'd ever be going back. The bedroom door opened and there was my mother looking bruised and flushed as if she'd been crying.

'Wake up, sleepy head,' she called cheerily.

After a quick breakfast of toast and jam I was soon seated in a huge, white stone sink in the kitchen being bathed by my mother. Through the window I could see some fishing boats bobbing about in a sea swell. Men were carrying boxes of fish up the pebbled beach to the road where a few horse-drawn carts were waiting. Flocks of hungry seagulls circled other men as they laboured over fishing nets at the edge of the bay.

Nearer to home, just outside the window, I could see a small kitchen garden filled with vegetable plants, which were shielded by a stone wall. There was a little path through the garden lined with what looked like seashells, all broken and crunched, while a large garden gnome in a red hat stood sentry near the gate. A crowd of starlings were busily strutting between the plants, pecking at the ground and competing noisily with each other for anything they could find to eat. My mother pointed to a robin, perched on the stem of a climbing rosebush outside, who was staring wistfully at us in anticipation of a treat. There was a warm and safe feeling about the big kitchen and the solid stone walls, which was a comfort after the traumatic events of the day before.

'Your Aunt Sheilis owns a family fish and chip shop and we are going along to help. Perhaps she'll let you work the chip machine. Would you like that?'

Suddenly feeling hungry I nodded and hurriedly rubbed my body dry with a thick patterned towel that smelt strongly of carbolic.

The fish and chip shop that my new aunt's family owned was in the middle of the high street and faced out over a headland towards the sea. It had a clean and shiny interior with lots of steel mountings on the fryers and spotless green plastic counters. My aunt's grandson, Stuart, a young man in his early twenties, was in charge and there were two local women who did the serving and cleaning.

Stuart was very friendly to me. He said he liked to be called Sty by his friends and he expected that now I would be his friend. He showed me how to peel the skin off potatoes so thinly that none of the flesh was wasted. Then I had to learn how to position a peeled potato on a machine that had serrated squares. When the handle was pulled down the potato was pressed through the squares and dropped down into a large bucket as chips ready to be cooked in the large fryers.

When Sty saw how helpful I was and how I did not shirk the work he whispered a secret to me. He told me that he would take me up the coast in his little boat, which had an outboard engine, to search in the sheltered bays for gold doubloons. He said that they had been washed ashore from sunken ships of the Spanish Armada that were shipwrecked during the reign of Elizabeth I, which I gathered was a long time ago. He explained that it all happened in the year 1588 when the King of Spain, Philip II, sent a huge fleet of ships and soldiers to invade England but was beaten back by English ships in the Channel. The scattered survivors of the Armada tried to return home by sailing north around Scotland but many were lost in fierce storms. Each ship was carrying gold coinage on board to pay the Spanish soldiers. It was such an enticing story that after so many years there could still be the odd gold coin washed up from a sunken hoard by the wild seas off the west coast. Sty told me not to tell anybody else so I didn't.

One very special day, when we were clearing up after the shop had closed, Sty drew me aside and withdrew a bright golden coin from his pocket. It was a doubloon. It was old, used and really heavy to hold, but it was beautiful to look at. Sty told me that he had one more hidden away. He said he planned to take me in his little boat if the weather was calm and clear on Sunday. We would search one of the numerous sheltered inlets which were blasted by the sea and overwhelmed when the furious storms from the Atlantic Ocean invaded the coast, sometimes depositing a doubloon in the sand and shingle.

At the end of the week, true to his word, Sty called round for me after breakfast and, with my mother's reluctant permission, we embarked in his small boat. Powered by the outboard engine, we went along the coast and up into one of the prettiest inlets I have ever seen. There were stony crags either side of us as we wound our way up the creek, which was filled with sparkling clear water. We could clearly see the bottom which, as we advanced further up the stream, was now only a few feet deep. At last we stopped and Sty cut the engine. He anchored the boat by throwing overboard a huge stone tied with a rope wound through a hole bored through its middle. After the roar of the little engine everything seemed appealingly quiet.

Sty took off his wellington boots and his socks, rolled up his jean bottoms and eased himself overboard. Then he took a garden rake from within the boat and began to rake the stony bed of the inlet with long deliberate movements. My job was to watch keenly for any sight of a glimmer or sparkle of yellow or silver. When Sty had finished raking one part of the stream he just pulled the boat along to another spot. At one point there was a huge rock in the centre of the stream, with a family of grey seals lying on top. They slid off as we drew near and lay submerged a short distance away, watching us with their heads only just sticking out of the water. I had never seen a seal up close and at first I was apprehensive since they seemed quite large but Sty said they wouldn't bother us as long as we left them alone.

As the day wore on I began to feel tired and hungry so we stopped and ate the home-cured ham and pease pudding sandwiches my aunt had made for us. Then we moved further up the creek and Sty started raking again. Just as I thought that we would never find anything I spotted a glint of something silvery between the stones near the bankside. At my shout Sty halted his raking and began to rummage amongst the stones and gravel where I thought I had seen something. Sure enough, after a moment or two Sty let out a shriek of delight and grasped something in his fingers. Clambering into the boat he showed me what he had found. It was a tiny silver cross with rounded ends and a minute figure of the crucified Christ on the front. On the reverse side there was some writing in a foreign language which Sty said was Spanish, the same as on his doubloons.

We were very excited by our find. Sty wanted me to have the cross but I told him that if my father saw that I had something valuable, he would only take it from me and sell it. Sty said he would keep it for me and hide it in a safe place along with his doubloons – and when I was older I could come and claim it.

By this time the day was much advanced and Sty's legs were blue with cold after so much time in the water. We returned back home in triumph but we kept our find a secret. The memory of that beautiful day searching for Spanish gold and silver remained in the forefront of my mind for many years. I fancifully imagined that when I grew up I would return to search for doubloons with Sty in the secret, sheltered Scottish waters, just like the characters in Robert Louis Stevenson's adventure book, *Treasure Island*. Only I never did.

Another thing Sty did for me was to introduce me to the wondrous grandeur of the Scottish Highlands. On another day off from preparing and selling fish and chips Sty took me on the back of his motorbike, which my aunt assured my mother was safe. We set out on a journey inland to explore the glens and mountains of the Scottish landscape. We rode up through misty valleys with sunbeams slanting through the mist and we picnicked on the crest of a hilltop that was surrounded by a mysterious sort of light, which gave a surreal aspect to everything around us. Sty said that the strange and beautiful light up high in the Highlands was due to all the moisture in the air. He also told me that somewhere in these mountains and crags that ringed the glen there lived a golden eagle, which he said was a great and elegant bird that could steal a lamb away in its massive talons.

'If we're lucky we'll see it today.'

We never caught sight of the eagle but we did see a kestrel hawk hovering expertly in the air before pouncing on its prey, probably a mouse or a shrew, in the long grass. We also spied a large, broad-winged bird high in the sky, no doubt watching us and wondering what we were up to. Sty said it was a buzzard, a bird like a big carrion crow that scavenged for dead things.

As the sun slid behind the mountains we collected the motorbike from where we had parked it and, as we made to leave, a soft mist enveloped us. It veiled but did not mask the august purity of the highland scene.

Suddenly it began to rain gently and, after the heat of the afternoon in the sheltered glen, its wetness was welcome on my face and the raindrops sweetened the taste of the highland air as they moistened my lips. It had been a marvellous day and I was thrilled by all I had seen. It was a day I would always remember and recall with nostalgia in later life when I visited the highlands on my own as a tourist. The warmth of Sty's friendship made the day so much more of an occasion and after I returned home I would remember his kindness to me. He treated me as if we were brothers.

During the weeks we stayed with my Aunt Sheilis, she told me stories about her brother William who was my maternal grandfather. He'd worked in the coalmines but after he married my grandmother and my mother was born he decided to emigrate to America in the hope of making a better life for his family. Once he was settled in a well-paid job at a steelworks in Pittsburgh, Pennsylvania, he had sent for them to join him but my grandmother was afraid to leave Blaydon and refused to go. He kept up correspondence for a number of years but eventually his letters ceased and she heard no more. My aunt showed me a faded sepia photograph of him on horseback when he was working on a ranch in Argentina and that was the last she had ever seen or heard of him so many years ago. It was a sad tale yet it excited my imagination to think what it might have been like to know him and hear the stories of his life. My aunt remembered him as being very lively and adventurous with a ready smile and loads of charm but, she said with a wry smile, he had a wild side too.

By now, I had found out that my mother was pregnant and I seemed to be more worried than ever about what would happen at home if we ever went back. Since I knew my mother would be resting at my aunt's because of her pregnancy I felt free to follow my own inclinations. Sometimes, when I had finished helping out at the fish and chip shop and Sty was busy with business things, I would wander off at will to explore the beach that extended beyond the bay. Just meandering along the sandy beach where it bordered the sea was an exhilarating experience. The tangy salty air was spiced with the smells of seaweed and flotsam. The immense sky seemed to go on forever and looked as if it could envelope and swallow you up into its total immensity. The wild cries of the kittiwakes as they swooped and dived in the turbulent air and the mesmerising cadence of the waves as they splashed against the shoreline enriched my senses and confirmed me as a beachcomber for the rest of my days.

In Victorian times sea air was thought to be therapeutic and the gentry began to popularize seaside resorts for health and recreation throughout the late nineteenth century and well into the twentieth. And like them, I now revelled in the invigorating scents brought ashore by the winds from the sea.

The sea breeze revived my flagging spirits, succouring my need for a comfort zone away from the fears and repressions of life at home. My body felt recharged by the spectacle around me and I felt energized with the same zest as the spray and spume of the waves as they erupted with sparkling highlights in the rays of the sun. My mother had bought me some sand shoes from the village store and my feet felt so light that I just had to run and run and, like the wading birds that took flight at my passing, I too felt I would be able to soar on the wind if I just made a little more effort.

Some days later there was consternation in the village because some of the household bins, including one at the fish and chip chop, were being raided by an animal intruder. Following a lot of speculation it was decided that the perpetrator was probably either a fox or a pine marten and a number of nasty steel traps were set. I hadn't told anyone but I knew almost positively that it wasn't a fox or a pine marten because I had seen the culprit. It was a cat, a really big cat that was grey with dark stripes. One night, I had seen it from my bedroom window when I was kneeling on my bed looking out at the sea in the moonlight. The cat looked fierce and very wild. Sty and I had talked about pets, cats and dogs because he was planning to buy a dog some day when he had time to train it. In answer to a question of mine he said he wouldn't have a cat because it might be vicious like some feral cats that people said lived in the area, mainly in the forest. I was sure that the animal I had seen in the moonlight was one of those wildcats, and from the heavy form of her body she looked to be pregnant.

I told Sty about the wildcat but said that I didn't want her to be trapped and killed, especially since she was pregnant. Sty said he would think about it and see what could be done. Later that day he told me to meet him in the public lavatories, which were in a stone building near the Stag's Head pub. When I got there Sty produced a large empty paint tin and told me to urinate in it. Then he did likewise and took the tin away with him. I was really mystified regarding what he intended to do but I trusted his judgement and expected that he would have something serious in mind.

Next day at the shop, Sty took me aside and told me that late at night, when no one was about and before the moon had risen in the sky, he had poured some of our urine on each of the three traps that had been set in order to prevent any wild animal from coming near them. He said it was a trick he'd learned from a fisherman whose dog had once been caught in a trap set by a gamekeeper in the nearby woods where he had taken his dog for walks. Sty said that he had it on good authority that no animal would go near a trap impregnated with human urine. Many times in later years I used this ploy when out walking in Northumberland and found traps set by farmers and game-keepers. Sty's plan seemed to work. Nothing was caught in the village traps and no more bins were raided, perhaps just because people started to take more care when disposing of their refuse. I kept on looking but I never saw the wildcat again.

Later in life I learned that the wildcat was very rare and mainly found in Scotland. They were classed as vermin because it was believed that they attacked lambs and slaughtered domestic fowl to supplement their food supply, especially when they had a litter of kittens to feed. Their virtual demise came when aristocratic landowners started to pay a bounty to gamekeepers for every wildcat they killed, and only a minority managed to survive in the farthest reaches of the Scottish Highlands. They all but joined the ranks of the wolf, the beaver and the elk, who were also hunted to extinction in their natural habitat in the British Isles. The wildcats, though, seem to be making something of a comeback. Michael, a friend of mine who lived at Powburn in Northumberland, said that he had once seen a wildcat when out walking at the foot of the Cheviot Hills and there are tales of a resurgence in the Scottish Borders. The one I saw that moonlit night in Scotland was a magnificent animal. I hope that she successfully delivered her kittens and raised them to maturity. To this day, I am obliged to Sty for his many kind actions but especially for his help in saving that wildcat of the Highlands.

We stayed an enjoyable and peaceful three weeks with my aunt, who said that she liked having us because she was often lonely with her son and daughter both away serving in the armed services.

My father had contacted the police who had traced us by questioning my grandmother. A local police officer called to see us and, after discussing the situation with my mother and aunt, said that we did not have to go back since my mother had not broken any laws. However, a few days later a catholic priest, no doubt informed through my father's parish, arrived at the door and told my mother that she was obliged for the good of her soul and her marriage to return home. Apparently my mother's pregnancy wasn't widely known before we left but my grandmother had told the police so that they could warn my father of the dangers of any further brutality against her. Now it was being used as the chief reason for her return. It was a wrench to leave and my aunt was heartbroken at our going.

As for me, I hadn't missed my father one little bit and had savoured the most delicious fish and chips I had ever eaten. With Sty I had explored Scottish waters for Spanish gold and had an adventure searching the Highland glens for sight of the elusive golden eagle. I had found a new friend in Sty and I would miss his happy company. However, I longed to see my grandmother again and eagerly looked forward to being with her.

A FAMILY AFFAIR

On our return from Scotland, there was no cheerful welcome home – there was only the strain of tension in the air. I had hardly been in the house for half an hour when my life once again assumed its repressive tone.

'Get yourself off somewhere,' my father barked at me. 'Me and your mother need to have a talk and I don't want you listening in.'

I hastened down to my grandmother's house with relief but I was worried about my mother being left alone with my father. I told my grandmother so and asked her why he was so cruel to us. She said that there were things that I was too young to know and that for the moment they were better left unsaid. Soon I was tucking in to a typical wartime dish of tripe and onions cooked in creamy milk and washed down by a glass of sarsaparilla, which my grandmother said was good for me. Everything seemed better at my grandmother's home because she was a very loving person. Even the food she cooked, which was necessarily basic because of wartime privations, tasted better than anything served up at home.

'Why did we have to leave our house at Axwell Park?' I asked as we sat relaxing after supper, listening to the wireless. This question had been bothering me for some time. I knew that I had been born in a house called Tynedale on the fringe of Axwell Park, but we had moved when I was young.

'There were things that happened and it was thought best that you all move back into the town.'

'Whatever happened?' I asked.

There was no response to my query. I had started to suspect that the move was somehow connected to our troubles as a family. Why else would we have moved from a lovely area to a terraced house in the backstreets of Blaydon-on-Tyne? Something must have happened and I thought that whatever that event was might lie at the heart of the way my father treated me. I decided that I had to wheedle the truth out of my grandmother because she was the only one who cared enough to realize that I needed to understand why my home life was so difficult. For the time being, however, she held her tongue.

Although my childhood and most of my boyhood was spent in and around Blaydon town, I have always felt drawn back to Axwell Park. It lies to the west of Blaydon and a mile inland from the River Tyne. The baronet, Sir Thomas Clavering, built a mansion called Axwell Hall on the estate in the late eighteenth century. After the death of the last family heir in 1893 the area went into decline and later began to be developed for residential purposes. In 1931 a line of very modern semi-detached villas were built adjoining Shibdon Road and backing on to wild parkland. The fourth house along was given the grand name Tynedale, which was arched in large letters in a glass panel above the front door. This was the house where I was born at around 10 a.m. on the 6 June 1934 in a large bed in the front bedroom. I was delivered by a famous general practitioner in the area, Dr Morrison, a land-owner and organic food enthusiast. To all intents and purposes I was regarded as a healthy baby and people remarked on my sweet disposition. I am told that I smiled a lot and slept soundly at nights.

I was aware from my earliest recollections that I shared my home life with a large black she-dog called Floss, who was my self-appointed guardian whenever my mother ventured out with me in my pram. If the pram was parked outside a shop or house, Floss would sit by the pram with one paw laid protectively over my body. The other animal companion of my babyhood was a silky-furred cat called Fluffy who would lie alongside me and purr in my ear. Both animals were wedding presents to my parents. Both disappeared within the first two years of my life. Floss went first. Apparently she was often slapped by my father with the sole of his slipper for misbehaving. One day his slippers disappeared and were discovered some weeks later buried in the garden's potato patch. Such a crime was deemed a capital offence and Floss was taken to be destroyed. Fluffy just left home, disappeared and was never found. This was perhaps a forewarning of things yet to come in my life.

I think I was mostly happy as a very young child but I soon learned to fear my father. I remember how upset I used to be whenever my mother went out in the evening and he had to change my nappy. He would hold me aloft with his hand grasping me by the left ankle whilst he cleaned me off. In the midst of my crying he would be saying things which I didn't understand but which gave me bad feelings nonetheless. When I was old enough to be able to walk freely without support I developed a distressing tendency of dislocating my left ankle and it required the attention of a doctor's home visit to reset my ankle. On one such occasion, my grandmother questioned the doctor and he said something about torn ligaments, which caused a terrific row in the house. She must have suspected that the problem was my father's fault. To this day my ankle has a tendency sometimes to just collapse without warning if my footwear does not offer enough support.

Even though I was very young, I started to feel that my father disliked me and missed no opportunity of saying or doing things to hurt me. There was an incident I remember when the coal fire in the sitting room went out. I had been given a large wooden spade from my grandmother so that I could dig in the garden. My father brought this spade out from the cupboard where it was kept, snapped it into pieces in front of me and used it to relight the fire. There were plenty of sticks in a box near the fire so I just could not understand why he needed my spade. When my mother arrived back home I was inconsolable about the loss of the spade. She couldn't understand what I was crying about since I was just two years old and my baby talk about what happened was incomprehensible. When I was older I began to suspect that there were things about our family that were not normal. The vibrations that underlaid our relationships were disturbingly negative.

It would be a couple of years until grandmother finally told me the truth. It was a Sunday afternoon and we were relaxing in front of the fire after lunch. I once again pleaded with her to tell me about what had happened to make us move from Axwell Park. She looked across at me without smiling and said that I must promise her that I would never ever repeat what she was about to tell me. She began speaking and there was a mournful tone to her voice that I had never heard before.

'In the time before your parents were married there was a lot of trouble between the families because your father's family were Catholics and your mother's wasn't. They insisted that she converted to Catholicism and even then they were very critical of her. Your dad's mother has never spoken to your mother to this day nor has she ever seen you. The O'Connors came from Ireland after the big famine when there was no work for them. They are a large family, twelve brothers and sisters, all of them born Irish except your dad and his youngest brother, Daniel.

'Well, against the wishes of myself and your Uncle John, your mother went ahead and married your father. They got no help from his family, not even a wedding present, and so it fell to us to help them get set up. Your Uncle John loaned them the money to buy the house your mother wanted at Axwell Park. When she first moved there she was lonely when your dad was at work and your father's brother, Dan, used to call on her. He taught her how to make small wagers, which were taken by illegal bookmakers such as the local milkman. Your mother and Dan grew very close but when you were born everything was fine until the local gossip got going. Suspicions grew out of all proportion until there was an unholy family hullabaloo and the priest was called in. Your mum and dad's marriage seemed to be in jeopardy for a while. There were many explosions of rage from your father and he called your mother and our side of the family some bad names and accused us of saying all manner of bad things about himself and his family.

'Now that we've talked this far about it, I'll tell you that he did say in one of his tempers that he was stuck with rearing a little bastard. Your Uncle John intervened at this stage and said that we would be happy to raise you ourselves. But the priest and your father's family would not allow that, mainly because your Uncle John is a member of the Church of England. I'm telling you this so that you can watch out for yourself and come to us if there is any trouble and particularly if he threatens you. Even if there is no truth in whispers they still linger on and can cause trouble. Nobody knows the truth of the matter but it does put you between the devil and the deep blue sea. Because of the gossip people scrutinized you as a baby with your hazel-coloured eyes and fair hair just like your dad's brother, Dan, whereas your parents have jet-black hair and blue eyes, as do both of your sisters.

'There were recriminations galore and then your parents had a long session with the parish priest, a special mass was said and there was some kind of reconciliation. But I'm sure that to this day your father thinks that you are not his son. He was jealous of his brother Dan anyway for getting to grammar school whilst he didn't, but now it has reached "bad blood" proportions, although on the surface everybody still pretends that all is well.

'The upshot of it was that your dad sold the Axwell Park house and moved your mother and you into a new place in Mary Street just up from the church where the curate could, some say, keep a check on things.

'So now you know what you face. You can come here to me anytime you feel threatened.'

After she had unburdened herself to me, I could see that she was visibly drained and soon she excused herself to go and lie on her bed for a Sunday nap.

I was shocked to a degree by what I had heard but intuitively I was relieved because I had long harboured suspicions of that nature and I can recall in later years my mother often saying that she 'had married the wrong brother'. From that point on, I couldn't but help noticing that whenever my Uncle Dan visited us he always made a point of hugging me, something my father never ever did. Dan had married a girl called Myrtle and had two sons by her, which everybody said were to someday train as priests, and they eventually did. I had always wanted a brother and often I longed to be part of that family rather than my own.

Although our two families seemed dominated by the high-toned moral principles of the Roman Catholic Church, on two occasions, when he thought no one was looking, I saw Uncle Dan pulling my mother into the hallway and kissing her passionately. Little boys sometimes see things they are not supposed to see, and they can have a lasting effect. The last time I saw my Uncle Dan I was in my forties and had two boys of my own. He hugged me affectionately, as he always did, and said he was sorry that he had not seen more of me over the years. When I looked at his face, I saw that he was crying.

Having been born there, Axwell Park became a place of refuge as I grew into a young lad and felt the need to get away from the backstreets of Blaydon. The wild wood of mature trees and bushes became my haven where I could keep in contact with nature. The park itself bordered on the wood and was overgrown with saplings and gorse. Most of it was impenetrable to anybody except small boys and animals. I frequently lost myself in this parkland as an antidote to the uptight atmosphere of tension and rigid rules at home.

School was no better for me and I continued to dodge it whenever I could. On one occasion when my Uncle John, who was away working in Doncaster, learned that I had played truant from school, he sent me a pound note and declared that I was 'a real lad at last'. At school, the children were almost afraid to blink because of the suffocating religious conditioning. I would steal English and Maths exercise books to work on alone at my grandmother's because I felt deprived of proper instruction – the school's priority was the rote-learning of the Catholic catechism and the all-important academic subjects were neglected. Poetry books and adventure readers also disappeared into my possession from the class library and joined my secret hoard at my grandmother's house. These types of books never seemed to be missed at school because they just weren't deemed important. I justified my stealing because I thought I would never be equipped to pass the eleven-plus examination and escape from this dreadful school if I didn't take matters into my own hands. I would return the books once I had achieved this precious goal.

In the meantime, on sunny days I would sit in the woods or by the lake at Axwell Park, reading poetry and extracts from classical books for children by authors such as Robert Louis Stevenson and John Buchan. A poem that I especially took to heart was 'Daffodils' by William Wordsworth because it aroused my own sense of wonder at all things natural. I longed to visit the Lake District to see the countryside that inspired Wordsworth. Lines from another famous writer, Sir Walter Scott, precisely expressed the way I felt about Axwell Park: 'Breathes there the man, with soul so dead, that never to himself hath said, This is my own, my native land!'

At school any misdemeanour or misbehaviour in class was deemed a sin and therefore an offence against God, which necessitated punishment by switches from a wooden cane against the palm of the hand. Some of the male teachers appeared to take a sadistic delight in administering a caning. Most of the women teachers were similarly disposed, and as well as the cane they enjoyed dispensing a hefty diet of moral righteousness. Unfortunately, due to a terrible administrative error at County Hall in Durham, myself and many local children had to spend another year at elementary school before we could take up our places in secondary school – it seems that there was a bureaucratic problem concerning eleven-plus entrants from independent church schools.

One teacher, a thin, middle-aged woman, habitually wore a pained expression as if nothing in this world ever pleased her. On one particular Monday morning in my final year, she stood sternly watching her class march into the classroom. When the class was assembled she said, 'Do not sit down. I have something extremely important to tell you before we begin to say our morning prayers.'

Then she embarked on a tirade of invective against our chief form of entertainment, the cinema. She began, 'It has come to my notice that there is an awfully bad film showing at the Plaza Picture House this week. It is called *Duel in the Sun* and it is not a fit film for children or indeed anybody to see who is a Christian. So I do not want anyone in my class going to see that film and I shall ask the priest, Father O'Hara, to speak the same message for your parents to hear at Mass tomorrow morning. Now sit down and get out you prayer cards.'

Well, for the rest of the morning we could think of nothing else. At playtime I got together with a group of boys and we made plans to see the film that evening. We were intrigued as to why she should want to ban us from seeing the film. Eddie

Robertson had seen it already with his older brother in a Newcastle cinema. Adopting a man-of-the-world demeanour, he told us that the film had sex in it. This made us all the more determined to see it, although one of the girls told her brother that if he went with us she would tell the teacher. He told her that he would thump her if she did and decided to come with us.

That night most of the boys and a few of the girls from our class were in the queue waiting for the cinema doors to open. The film proved a popular success with all of us since it was a decent Western starring popular actors (including Gregory Peck), and it had lots of action scenes and fighting. There was a girl in the film who was very beautiful and there was a scene where she was cuddling and kissing the hero. The door then closed, suggestively, leading the newspapers to nickname the film 'Lust in the Dust'. In fact, this was lost on us. We tended to ignore such scenes and were usually either talking or throwing paper missiles at each other while they were going on. We went to the pictures for the action scenes; we were not yet really interested in that mysterious thing called sex.

The next morning in the playground a few of us were discussing why our teacher should have wanted to ban us from watching such an enjoyable film. We could only suspect that something to do with the relationship between the man and woman had offended our teacher's strict religious beliefs, but as none of us shared them, in the end we decided that she was an oddball. However, as we did not quite understand what had gone on, we did feel a sort of shame at having watched the film.

Some days later my father demanded to know if I had seen 'that film' as he called it. With my heart thumping wildly I lied and denied that I had seen it, which only made matters worse. Now I felt the fear of being exposed as a liar as well as the vestiges of shame. I don't think he believed me but on this occasion he didn't beat me. I think it gave him enough satisfaction to know that his questioning had frightened me.

One thing I did learn from going to such a cold, unfriendly elementary school was to fight back against bullying, which was rife. We couldn't report any bullying to a teacher, especially the male teachers, without being labelled as an effete cry-baby, a funker. So, thanks to one of my friends, Billy Murphy, I learned how to fight. Billy's father had worked as a boxer in fairground booths and he had passed his skills on to his son. Billy taught me the hard way, spending sessions boxing with me. He showed me how and where to punch an opponent to have the greatest effect.

My first confrontation was with an arch bully called Brian Byers, an older boy who delighted in striking boys from behind, knocking them down and then kicking them. One day I saw him coming at me out of the corner of my eye and so I turned and moved in close enough to land a thumping uppercut to his face. Taken totally by surprise he fell back, bleeding profusely from the nose. To seal my triumph he began to cry. He never tried to hit me again.

However, I was still frequently punched by a boy called Frank McNally who sat behind me in class. He was careful to only strike me when the teacher had her back turned. One afternoon when he punched me yet again I decided that enough was enough. I stood up from my bench desk, turned around, grabbed him by the hair and proceeded to hit him a rain of blows without stopping to let him recover. Suddenly I was grabbed from behind by the teacher, a burly woman called Miss Scott, who dragged me in front of the class and caned me several times while calling me a thug. I didn't care. I didn't even feel the thwacks of the cane because I was glowing with elation at having overcome a sneak bully. He was so battered by my onslaught that he had to spend the rest of the afternoon recuperating with the school nurse in the medical room. Billy said that he was delighted at my performance and took me to see his dad, a huge man with cauliflower ears and a twisted nose who shook hands with me and advised me to always 'hit them in the bread basket' – the stomach.

I escaped my own personal school of hard knocks that year when the administrative error at County Hall was cleared up and I was finally judged to have passed the eleven-plus, largely due to the extra work I had done myself. I was so glad to be free at last from St Joseph's Elementary School. My father tried to insist that I should go to the Roman Catholic grammar school, St Cuthbert's in Newcastle upon Tyne, but I protested that I'd had enough of religious instruction. I wanted to learn real knowledge. Surprisingly he gave way and, even more surprisingly, he didn't beat me. My mother said it was because if I'd gone to St Cuthbert's he would have had to pay the money for my fares to Newcastle each day. It satisfied his mean streak that I could walk to Blaydon Grammar School. This suited me just fine because the school was opposite Axwell Park.

FRIENDS IN THE PARK

My whole life changed when I went to the grammar school and my attachment to Axwell Park became even stronger.

Before we left the area when I was a young boy, I had already become familiar with the parts of the park that backed on to our garden at Tynedale. My friend from along the street, Robin Patterson, who was about the same age as myself, would join me in exploring the woodland and streams adjacent to where we lived. We played all kinds of games together and one day in early summer we found a huge field that was overgrown with tall grasses. It was full of brilliantly coloured butterflies and we wore ourselves out trying to catch them in our hands. There was a rutted cart track leading into the field, which was bordered by aged trees on three sides and by the upper reaches of the lake on the lower side. We decided that the field was our secret territory and we spent hours exploring the area and watching the birds hunting for insects to feed their nestlings, which we could sometimes hear crying as the parent bird returned to the nest with food. Soon we knew where all the brooding birds had set their nests and each time we came to the field we quietly checked the growth and health of the nestlings.

After we moved house to live in Blaydon I remembered those halcyon days and would often make my way back to the park when I wanted to escape the miserable atmosphere at home. On one particular morning in the summer holidays before I was due to start grammar school, I was sitting near the middle of the field just looking at the wild flowers, such as dandelions, buttercups, wild poppies, clover and my special favourite, cowslips. Sometimes a bird – a finch or a meadow pipit – would be startled by my presence as they foraged around the field for beetles and grubs. It was soothing also to watch the bees busily gathering nectar and to listen to their melodic humming. But on that sunny day the tranquillity was shattered when I heard a clomping and creaking, and a pounding of the ground. The noise seemed to be coming my way.

I stood up immediately and looked above the tall grasses. A huge horse was pulling a large farming contraption, which began cutting the grass. Seated on the top of the machine was a big man wearing a cap and a long shirt that came down to his knees, which were covered by thick-looking trousers. When he spotted me standing in the middle of the field he pulled the horse to a stop and called for me to come to him. He didn't seem to be angry and I could see that he was smiling. When I got up to him he called down to me from his high seat on the machine.

'Now, young lad, what are you doing in my field when I'm setting about cutting the hay?'

He looked to be a kindly man and so I had no hesitation in telling him of my interests.

'I'm sorry to interfere with your work but I like to come here among the birds and the flowers because it's peaceful.'

He regarded me quizzically and then, aware of the work yet to be done, he abruptly said, 'Well, you'd best be off now in case we cut your tail off.'

I refused to be put off and tried again to get through to him that I had a genuine sense of belonging in his field.

'Please can I stay and watch you,' I said. 'There's a skylark nesting in the field and she's got young 'uns and I can show you where her nest is so you don't crush it.'

'Well now,' he said, taking off his cap and scratching his head. 'I suppose you can stay as long as you keep out the way of this machine. You can stand where yon nest is if you like so I'll see to miss it.'

By now I was paying attention to his horse, which had turned its head to have a look at me.

'What kind of horse is it?' I asked.

'He's a shire horse and he does the hard work on this farm. His name is Benny. I'll be stopping in a minute and if you like I'll let you sit up on Benny. Would you like that?'

I nodded my head. Flushed with excitement I ran to stand next to the skylark's nest. She flew off as soon as I got there but the nestlings, five of them, were still crammed in the nest.

Mr Bramer, as I later came to know him, was as good as his word and let me sit on Benny, holding on tight to his halter. I patted his massive neck and Mr Bramer told me to say Benny's name to him so that he'd know the sound of my voice and that I meant him no harm.

I had a wonderful day watching the hay being cut and trussed by the machine. Afterwards the field looked really bare except for the small area of grass and weeds that Mr Bramer had left for the skylark to raise her brood. Later in the afternoon, when I thought it was time to go home, I called out to Mr Bramer, who was stacking the trusses of hay, to let him know that I was leaving. He came across to me and, after asking my name and where I lived, he said that I could come up to his farm to see the swallows nesting in his barn.

'There are some owls there too if you'd like to see them.'

I thanked him and ran home to tell my mother. Later in the week I went to Mr Bramer's farm. He was working on some farm machinery in the yard when I eventually found the place. He seemed genuinely pleased to see me and, stopping what he was doing, he took the time to show me around and I was able to meet Benny again, standing massive and majestic in his loose box.

I was thrilled when I entered the barn to see the beautifully coloured swallows fast-winging acrobatically through the air to reach their nests of dried mud and grasses and feed their young. Mr Bramer directed me up a ladder inside the barn to a shelf in a corner where two white owlets, all covered in fluffy white feathers, were leaning out expectantly for the next feed. I didn't go too close because I was being carefully observed by an enormous white barn owl perched on a nearby beam.

Mr Bramer showed me his pigs, some of which had litters of piglets, and I especially enjoyed standing in the chicken shed looking at some large hens called wine dots, a type I hadn't seen before. I got the impression, though, that the large rooster wasn't too happy about my presence, which was fair enough since he was the boss bird.

Mr Bramer said I could come to visit any time and before I left Mrs Bramer gave me a piece of apple pie and a drink of homemade sweet lemonade. I really felt at home there and I loved seeing the animals. I decided that next time I came I would bring an apple for Benny.

From that time on I would use Mr Bramer's farm as an additional refuge when my life at home grew unbearable.

I have always been drawn to wild places, even if they have been turned into more orderly parks. Axwell Park is such a place. The woods, the lake and the streams were carefully landscaped to enhance the environment for those who live in the expensive private housing that surrounds the park. It had pathways and seats in convenient sites and there was a bridge over the lake. This led to a wide green expanse of grassland that had been thoroughly developed as a wildlife habitat and was dominated by a towering horse chestnut tree. In the very far corner of the field there were two grass tennis courts. Nevertheless, for a young boy living in the suburban backstreets of Blaydon, Axwell Park still had enough natural wilderness to explore and savour.

On some sunny summer days, as I lazily stretched out on the grass by the lake, alone with my thoughts, I would often hear laughter coming from adult couples playing mixed doubles on the courts. The sounds of such merriment made me feel empty inside as it contrasted so markedly with the way my mother and father related to each other. Cheerful laughter, more especially the uninhibited kind, was a singularly rare commodity in our house; in fact, it was probably viewed as a sin or likely to give rise to one.

Part of my family's domestic routine at weekends involved social gatherings in which we would visit or be visited by one or two families from my father's side. From a child's point of view, they tended to be boring affairs where the adults shared reminiscences or gossiped about the failings of other family members who were not there. Meanwhile, children were admonished to be on their best behaviour so as to provide a showcase of family integrity. Great fuss had to be made of the younger children's toilet skills and often commode pots were passed around for the assembled company to witness the proficiency of a particular child's bowel movement.

I kept a low profile at these sessions, as did most of the other children, but not Harold. He was the six-year-old son of Uncle Patrick and Aunt Molly. Uncle Patrick held the post of senior staff sergeant at Sandhurst, the British Army's elite training college for officers. He was a frightening man. He had a shaved head, small dark eyes and a thin moustache above his lip. It was rumoured within the family that he beat his wife who had been incarcerated in an asylum several times, apparently for treatment of nervous depression. But his son, Harold, was his pride and joy. Whenever I looked at Harold I felt a little shudder. He resembled the shape of the Neanderthal children, as depicted in my history picture books. He had a large head and virtually no neck, a jutting jaw and little piggy eyes. His body appeared to be fashioned from a single piece of solid rock.

However, I'm not one to judge by looks alone, and it was his crude behaviour rather than his physical appearance that gave most cause for concern. Harold was being educated at the Army's expense at a private boarding school run by an order of ecclesiastical brothers but his manners left much to be desired. When sitting at the table he would suddenly say 'Fuck' – although prompted by nothing in particular – and repeat this word several times until he had everyone's attention. He would then display an evil, gap-toothed grin. By this time his mother, Molly, would be in outraged hysterics and order him to go to the bathroom, where he would commence to yell, within everyone's earshot, 'Shit and piss to you lot of flea bags.' This tirade would continue until his father would stick his head into the hallway and shout in the direction of the bathroom, 'Attention! Shuuuuurrrr up!' Then peace would reign again except for the suppressed giggles of the children.

At one of these family gatherings my mother took along my newborn sister, Gloria, the younger of my two sisters. At one point Molly, who was wearing a nasty bruise on her face, insisted on nursing the baby. She carried her over to where

Harold was sitting and said, 'Look, Harold, wouldn't you like a nice baby sister like her?'

'Cunt,' said Harold, without a trace of shame.

This caused another scene in which Molly accused her husband of deliberately teaching Harold bad things. Uncle Patrick's reply, made in front of the entire family, was, 'Shut your stupid whingeing mouth or I'll shut it for you.'

One time just after Christmas, crackers were provided at the dinner table for the children. I pulled mine with one of the other children and won a tin whistle. After the meal, Harold was prevailed upon by his father to recite a verse or two from some military poem, which I think was Tennyson's 'The Charge of the Light Brigade'. I was playing about with my whistle when suddenly it blew, causing Harold to halt in mid recitation.

Furious, he turned on me and screamed, 'You horrible little man. I shall cut your balls off if I hear another sound from you!'

Later, after Uncle Patrick had left with his family, talk amongst the remaining company turned to Harold and it was their unanimous consensus that the boy was a 'chip off the old block' whose language owed much to the influence of his father. There was great concern expressed for Molly whose temperament in no way suited such a family. Eventually Harold, at the age of twelve, was sent to Army school and I heard nothing of him again. Aunt Molly suffered several nervous breakdowns and on medical advice was finally taken into long-term nursing care.

Exposure to such incidents as these started me thinking about what kind of family I had inherited on my father's side. They

were certainly a rum lot. My paternal grandfather had apparently
taken upon himself the duty, no doubt strongly motivated by his
religion, of breeding for Ireland. As well as the twelve children
he had by his first wife, who died at the tender age of fifty-six, he
then had two more children by his second wife, whom he had
initially hired as his housekeeper. The household in which my
father and his siblings grew up was spartan to say the least. Some
of my uncles, who would sometimes confide in me during parties,
reported that there was never enough food to go round. Their
usual diet consisted chiefly of potatoes, cabbage and home-baked
bread. Butter and jam were luxuries but seasonal gluts of apples
made up for deficiencies in other areas. Like many immigrant
Irish families, they existed on a shoestring and the care of the
undernourished children was sacrificed as the parents continued
the prevailing dogma of unfettered procreation.

I only got to know a few of my father's brothers, but they
showed marked dissimilarities. Aside from Patrick the military
man, there was John, who was probably the brother with the
most pleasant disposition. He dabbled in vaudeville as a song-
and-dance man – he once offered to teach me how to tap
dance – but when that fell through he had to take employment
at the cokeworks. There he contracted a respiratory disease,
which killed him when he was only forty-two. Chris was a
layabout cadger who gambled away every penny he got his
hands on. He also drank a great deal.

Daniel, the youngest brother, was the star of the family. An
intelligent high-achiever, he gained a degree in science from

Strawberry Hill College on the outskirts of London and became a teacher. When the Second World War started he enlisted in the Army and was commissioned as a second lieutenant. He went on to lead a team of soldiers who parachuted into Crete to help the partisans in their fight against the German occupation. Later, when he and his commando force were threatened with capture, he led them to safety along the twelve-mile long Samaria Gorge towards the coast. Once there, they were picked up by a British Navy destroyer and transported to safety. Daniel would always take an interest in me, which was not a surprise in the light of what I was learn when I was older. Years later, while on holiday in Crete, as a token of respect for Dan I walked the twelve miles of the gorge with my son, Christopher. By the time we had finished my feet had been reduced to bleeding tatters.

At these family gatherings my father hardly said a word and was especially deferential to Tony, his elder brother, who had a degree in engineering. My father had brought shame on the family by getting mixed up with a Protestant English girl and was not well regarded in contrast to the 'stars' of the family – Tony, John and Dan.

The women in my father's family were also very different from each other. Irene was a calm lovable woman who married my favourite uncle on that side of the family, a debonair sportsman called Terence who had competed in the 1948 Olympics. At parties he had the patience to spend a lot of time talking to me and answering my questions. He was the person who first awakened my interest in cricket and he gave me my first cricket bat, which was almost too heavy for me to lift, let alone use, but his intentions were good. I also knew two of my father's sisters, Florence and Kathleen. Florence trained as a nanny and moved away to work in the south of England. Kathleen had a hypertensive personality and was given to hysterical episodes.

Like my father, Kathleen was steeped in the punitive and judgemental side of Catholicism. I remember being told by one of my uncles about the depth of her religious guilt. One day after attending early morning Mass she was so engrossed in chatting with a friend as they left the church that she forgot to dip her hand in the holy water and make the sign of the cross. This bothered her all day and that night, as she ascended the stairs on her way to bed, she had a vision of the devil. At this point, thinking the story was being related for amusement, I laughed, only to receive a hard clout on the ear from my father and several reproving looks from the rest of the adults. My uncle continued, saying that the parish priest was informed about the vision and then the bishop had to be notified. Consequently, a Dominican father who was trained as an exorcist was despatched to carry out a special blessing on Kathleen and the house.

Most of family, including Kathleen, had been born in a town called Mullingar in County Westmeath, central Ireland. Whenever she came to visit our family she was always full of warning stories to us children about the dangers of opening the door to strangers after dark. 'You must be careful after you've looked at their face to check their feet for cloven hooves, as they could be a devil after your soul.'

I remember my sisters becoming frightened at these stories and so my father taught them a prayer to say each night to their guardian angel.

Quirky aunts were not confined to my father's side of the family, as I found out from my Aunt Mary Ann, my grandmother's sister. She told me of a maiden aunt of hers who developed an infatuation for Earl Kitchener of Khartoum. Kitchener drowned in 1916 when the HMS *Hampshire*, on which he was travelling on a government mission to Russia, struck a mine and sank. From that day on, my aunt told me, her maiden aunt vowed never to eat fish again as a tribute to her hero and she kept her promise until she died.

As a child I was surrounded by so many prejudices, superstitions and religious beliefs, as well as some strange adults with misguided child-rearing practices, that I'm surprised that my own outlook on life managed to escape relatively unscathed. With the benefit of hindsight, I sometimes wonder how I managed to hang on to my sanity. I think that even as a child I was able to offset the bad things, the horrors in my life, with my attachment to nature and the wild creatures of the woods and hedgerows. I really believe that animals have a way of helping a person to make meaningful connections with the realities of life that most people cannot achieve alone.

I am obliged to a few teachers who inspired and guided me in the path of learning, but before I went to grammar school,

I think I learned more insights from nature than I did from family or school. The repressive religious regime at elementary school did almost as much as my home life to dampen and break my youthful spirit. Whenever I thought I was just having a good time, the adults around me would tell me I was committing a sin, so in the end all pleasure seemed to be tainted with sinful attributes and all things happy were reduced to the miserable.

Even having a sense of humour seemed to place me at a perpetual disadvantage. Once, during a rounders match in the schoolyard, a classmate turned to me and said something funny and I laughed out loud. Instantly the teacher, a man called Wordsworth, marched across the yard and slapped me hard in the face. He didn't say it on this occasion but the usual comment on bad behaviour at school was that it was an offence against God and needed to be punished. I wondered just what kind of behaviour did God expect of me? And what kind of God was it who allowed children to be abused in this way?

A much more serious incident took place that gave me severe qualms about exactly what Godliness entailed. Now that I was twelve and due to start grammar school in the autumn, my father decided that I should learn how to serve God at Holy Mass and he prevailed upon the parish priest to enlist me as an altar boy. I was given no choice in the matter. This meant rising early every day and attending church at 8 a.m. for early morning Mass in order to learn the ritual moves required of the altar boys. Towards the end of my first week, I served Mass with an older boy who gave me guidance. Once the Mass was over the older boy, who was at St Cuthbert's, raced off to catch the bus for Newcastle. I was left to help the priest clear up. When I'd finished I changed out of my cassock into my jacket and was just about to leave when the priest, a man in his forties or thereabouts, stopped what he was doing and stood in front of me.

'Now you need to learn to do as you are told as part of the discipline of the church. Do you understand that, Denis? And your first duty is to serve me,' he said.

He then closed the vestry door and, turning to face me, exposed his genitals. He beckoned me to come to him and I froze on the spot. Panic seared through me and I bolted past him for the door. It was a struggle to open the heavy wooden door and I felt terror as I heard him coming up behind me. At last the door swung wide and I fled. When I reached the church exit I turned and looked back. He was standing watching me with a devilish smile on his face which gave me the shivers. I ran from the church and didn't stop until I reached the town square. There I hunched down on my haunches against the wall next to the greengrocer's display tables laden with fruit and vegetables. Now I had a fearful problem. Who should I tell? What should I do?

I went home and in a breathless rush told my mother. She was busy in the kitchen at the time and my disclosure had a serious effect on her because she came to face me and said, 'Are you absolutely sure this is what happened or did you imagine it?'

Adamantly I asserted that I had told her only the truth.

She said, 'You must not go back there again and see that you are never ever alone with that priest.'

I went upstairs and started going through my comics, trying to put the matter out of my head.

At about 3 a.m. in the morning I was rudely awakened by my father pulling me out of bed. As I struggled to come awake I could see that he was in a vile mood.

'What you told your mother about the priest this morning, that was a lie, wasn't it? It was you trying to get out of serving Mass, wasn't it?' he whispered harshly, his angry face close to mine.

'No, I did not lie. It happened like I said,' I stuttered.

'You lying little bugger. I'll belt your arse for lying to me!'

And with that he grabbed me by the hair and started laying into me with his hand, calling out 'Liar, liar, liar' as he did so.

Suddenly I managed to wrench free of him and screamed, 'I did not lie. If you force me back there I'll tell everybody at school what happened, I'll tell the neighbours and I'll tell my Uncle John and he'll tell the police.'

He reared back at this, his faced twisted in an odd way that I hadn't seen before. But I guessed what he was thinking. His precious, obsessive and unswerving belief in his religion meant that he thought that the Church was pure and infallibly good. He was imagining what would happen if people discovered that a priest, the anointed of God, was a paedophile. To my relief he turned away and headed back to his bedroom, where I soon heard my mother asking him questions.

I was shaken. I knew that the last thing he would ever do would be to defend me, and he would never take my word against anybody else's in any situation. But I was glowing with satisfaction that at last I had succeeded in stopping his violence against me. To my horror he appeared at my bedroom door again. I held my breath, not knowing what to expect.

'You keep your mouth shut about this! You are to tell nobody. Do you understand?'

I nodded agreement and he left. From then onwards the only time I went to church was with the school for Benediction on Thursday and for the mandatory family Mass on Sunday.

THE WHITE CAT

tarting on the Monday after this weekend, I was told by my father that I would be going with him to help out when he did extra jobs in the evening. On Monday evening we would be going to the Scotswood Co-operative store to do some extra work for the manager, Mr Grange, and I would be my father's 'helping hand', as it was put to me.

I trembled at this development. Alarm bells began to ring in my head. Why Scotswood? To get to the place of work it would be necessary to cross the massive Scotswood Bridge from which I had been chased, along with others, many times by the Bridge Keeper. He was a rough old man who carried a red flag which he used to control the traffic and also sometimes to hit any boy that he thought was up to no good. My friends and I had felt that stick against our legs several times in the past when we were caught birdwatching under the bridge. The River Tyne flowed fast and wide under the bridge and I would always give a little shudder when I thought of what it would be like to fall into that mass of cold water that held many secrets in its murky depths.

Once my grandmother told me a story about a nearby family in which the man of the house took a serious dislike to the black cat that belonged to the family. He swore that he would kill the cat. An old lady who lived there, the family's maternal grandmother, told him, 'If you attempt to kill a black cat then you will yourself die by the same means. Be very careful because all cats have nine lives and black cats, in particular, are said to have been gifted with power from the Dark Side of Nature.'

But the man only grinned and made jokes of the old woman's words.

In November of that year the nights were wintry cold, which was when the man took his chance to kill the black cat. He placed the cat along with a heavy stone in a hessian bag and secured the bag with a rope tied around the open end. He then went to Scotswood Bridge and threw the bag into the deepest waters of the Tyne. He walked home and gleefully began telling the family what he'd done when he noticed the cat, soaked to the skin, sitting on a stool by the fire and licking itself dry. No one knew how the cat had got out of the bag but from that time on the man was terrified of that cat and would go nowhere near it.

About a week later, on a Saturday night after a drinking session in the public houses along the Newcastle Quayside, the man caught the last train home. However, he did not disembark as expected at Blaydon railway station where his younger brother was waiting to help him home, knowing that he would be the worse for wear due to the amount of alcohol he regularly drank on these occasions. The man was not on the train. In fact, he was never seen alive again.

Some days later his drowned body washed up on the Newburn side of the river. The police believed that he had attempted to leave the train when it had stopped for a short while on the railway bridge over the river before pulling into the station. It was suspected that he had fallen into the waters and drowned.

After relaying this tale my grandmother sternly told me to always greet black cats with respect and never to hurt one. But, of course, she didn't know then how deeply I would come to adore all cats and that I would spend a great deal of my life caring for them – and one singular cat called Toby Jug in particular. I have met and befriended many black cats in my life and they have always acknowledged my salutations with a muted cry or a cordial flick of the tale.

There are many other tales involving drowning in the river by Scotswood Bridge, both accidental and deliberate. At times the river surface assumes a sort of dark sheen that looks hostile and very dangerous. I never relished the thought of crossing the bridge at the best of times, but the thought of crossing it in the dark after work, in the company of a man whom I knew hated me, made me particularly nervous. I decided that if we were alone on the bridge, I would go ahead of my father to be out of his reach in case he tried to throw me into the river.

For two weeks I worked at the Co-operative for three nights a week between seven and nine o'clock. I fetched and carried tools and wood for my father as he worked. Each night as we walked home not a word was exchanged. On two of the nights the bridge was shrouded in fog as we walked home and on each foggy night I ran ahead and waited for him at the other side. I was glad when the job was over. He never again asked me to help him when he worked overtime, which left a suspicion lurking in my mind as to why he had asked me in the first place.

Mr Grange, the store manager, made a great deal of fuss over me and on the last night he gave me half a crown – a lot of money to a boy back then – for being such a hard worker. On one of the nights, he called me over and asked if I liked cats. I said that I did but my father did not allow them.

'Well, we'll see about that,' he said, booming with a loud voice that was in keeping with his large size.

Then he ushered me along a corridor to a store cupboard, which he opened to reveal a litter of snow-white kittens. I loved them all at first sight. The kittens were about five weeks old and Mr Grange said I could choose one and take it home if I liked. I told him again that much as I just adored the kittens I was sure my father would not allow me to keep one. At this Mr Grange said, 'Well, let's go and ask him.'

With that he charged along the corridor to where my father was working. Taken aback by Mr Grange's hearty manner my father was at first at a loss for words. It was then that I had a sudden inspiration. Knowing that he wouldn't indulge my liking for pet animals I blurted out, 'My mother has always said she would love to have a white cat!'

My father looked at me and then at Mr Grange, who was grinning from ear to ear.

'Very well, then, pick a kitten to please your mother and we'll take it home as a surprise for her.'

I hurried back to the store cupboard and knelt down beside the box holding the kittens. They were all lovely but one little male kitten stood out from the rest. He looked as if he wanted to be the leader of the pack. I chose him and Mr Grange brought a cardboard box of just the right size to fit him into, along with some straw to keep him warm for the journey home.

On our arrival my father said to my mother, 'He has a present for you.' She looked mystified.

I presented her with the box, which was fastened shut with some string tied around to keep it secure. When she opened the box and saw the white kitten a look of delight crossed my mother's face as she exclaimed 'What have we here?'

Apprehensive of my father standing there, I interjected hastily, 'You always said you would love a white cat didn't you, Mother?'

My mother gave me a sharp look and quickly appraised the situation.

'Well, yes I did. Thank you both for this lovely present. He'll always be safe with me.'

She wanted to reassure me that the kitten would be safe from my father.

'Now, what shall we call him?' she continued. 'Help me pick a name for him.'

At this juncture my father disappeared and I was left with my mother who worriedly whispered, 'Has he been all right with you?'

I nodded and didn't say more for fear of being overheard. The white kitten was now out the box and lying comfortably in true cat fashion on my mother's lap as she sat in her chair by the fireside. I tried to think of an appropriate name for the kitten. I came up with Blanco, Chalkie and Snowy, trying out the names on my mother to see what she thought of them.

'They are very good names,' she said. 'Any one of them would do.' And then she had an inspiration. 'Do you recall there was an item in the newspapers lately about a baby polar bear that was born at London Zoo? Do you remember what it was called?'

'Brumas!' I almost shouted as the memory of the picture of the cuddly little white bear came back to mind.

'Then his name shall be Brumas,' my mother said, smiling.

Meanwhile, the kitten, who still retained the blue eyes of kittenhood, looked on and appeared quite content to have been given a special name.

As I stood up to go for my supper I heard a creak of the floorboards in the hallway as someone moved. Undoubtedly my father had been listening surreptitiously to what we had said. I was pleased that he had overheard my mother choosing the name for the little white cat – it made the kitten seem more obviously hers. Perhaps then Brumas would be safe in this house. I decided to be very careful not to attach him too closely to me, because that could put his life in danger.

I offered my mother the half-crown that Mr Grange had given me because I knew she was always short of money. She thanked me with a lovely smile but said that I should keep it to save for something that I would really like. What I really wanted was a bicycle. I had yearned for one for years but the timing never seemed to be right to ask for one. I thought perhaps this year I could ask for a bicycle for my birthday, especially if I raised some of the money towards its cost.

Brumas proved to be an exceptional cat and lived with my mother for seventeen years. Although he was allowed to roam free he managed to avoid the fate of many of the other cats in our area, who were run over on the busy roads. I loved him, but as I had promised to myself, I kept my distance. I was right to be wary of my father's continuing cold-heartedness towards animals. On a summer morning soon after Brumas had arrived, I saw him go up a ladder to drag out a starling's nest, complete with fledglings, from a gap under the roof of our house. I was filled with despair to see the nest and its occupants hurled into the back lane and to hear the distressed cries of the mother bird as she circled the smashed nest. Unfortunately there was nothing I could do to save them. As far as I know, though, my father never turned his hatred towards Brumas – making sure that he was never thought of as my cat seemed to work.

My life at home, school and church during my early boyhood generated a yearning for a happier, normal sort of life which I hoped to able to live one day, but I knew that to attain it I would have to get away from the circumstances in which I was presently trapped. This endeavour was now a preoccupation of my mind. Gaining a place at grammar school opened up new vistas for me, which I was determined and happy to pursue, but the secret place in the woods would never be far from my mind and I would still retreat there whenever I needed to embrace nature in all its myriad forms.

At weekends when my homework was finished and the weather was pleasant I would steal away to languish by the lake near the slim wooden bridge, which afforded me a close-up view of life at the water's edge. It was here, on a long, sunny day in spring, that I took to watching a stickleback in the water. He wore his mating plumage, with dark stripes and spines on his back and an iridescent turquoise underside, as he skilfully weaved his nest of water weed. He was very meticulous in his attention to detail, trying to create as attractive a nest as possible so that a female would come to lay her eggs there for him to fertilize. Once this had been accomplished, his role would be to spend much of his time guarding the nest containing the young from predators, like a really loving father. Eventually the young would leave the nest to begin a new life and he would retire and die.

Meanwhile, he spent a great deal of time and concentration selecting only the freshest looking greenery and pulling together the strands of weed. Watching him, which I did for well over an hour, I could tell that he was exercising careful judgement as to whether each piece of weed seemed right for one particular spot or should go somewhere else. I was convinced that I was viewing a natural work of art in the making. This elegant tiny creature, created and designed by the evolution of nature, was an inspiration to behold. It was soulfully uplifting to observe him attending to his decreed purpose, his destiny if you like, without any need for guidance from external sources. He knew what to do because it was what he'd been created to do. If he did it well then he and his offspring would survive. If he didn't do it well, if he made a hash of it, then his survival and that of his species might or would be in jeopardy. This was his moral code, his responsibility for the continuance of his kind – so simple to understand and follow.

If I had voiced any such thoughts to my father, to teachers at my school or to the priest at our church, I would have been condemned as a heretic for ascribing responsible sentience – the ability to perceive or feel things – to a being other than a human. Yet I knew it to be true because I had seen it happening with my own eyes. Of course, cynics might accuse me of anthropomorphism – projecting human qualities on to animal behaviour. But I have always believed that such a charge is invalid since my observations have always led me to recognize that animals, especially mammals and birds, feel pain and experience anxiety, have concerns about survival and need to mate, much as humans do. Pet animals often express sentiments of loving affection and even sympathy for their human guardians. Those people who do not believe that animals are really aware or can feel things can give themselves the licence to do anything they wish to an animal, including vivisection.

Much of what I think about nature to this day was worked out in those childhood times in Axwell Park, observing the rhythms of nature in so many different forms. I loved the animals and birds of the wild wood and lakeside, which had become a kind of second home, and one far preferable to my other one. And because I loved them, I made the effort to understand them, just like I would try to understand the thoughts and needs of my friendly little cat, Toby Jug, in later life. In ancient Chinese philosophy man (and no doubt woman, too) was considered to be part of the natural world and able to benefit from its wisdom and exist totally in harmony with it. I didn't know much about Chinese philosophy back then, but I came to the same conclusion.

I started to make friends with boys who lived in the houses around Axwell Park. They had seen me in the park on numerous occasions but they weren't sure about me at first because they suspected that I went to the Catholic school, while they were from the Church of England elementary school. The divisive effects of religion were apparent even at this early age and many were the days when I witnessed 'Sod Fights' taking place in the streets around the two schools. This consisted of the antagonists pulling up the clumps of weeds growing between the cobbles of the unpaved streets and throwing them at each other to the sound of accusatory war-cries such as 'Catholic rats' and 'Proddy dogs'. Once the boys of Axwell Park discovered that I'd been born in the locality and that my religious views were as neutral as their own, we got along just fine.

Many of these boys became lasting friends of mine. 'Tann' was my best friend. His given name was Alan but no one except his mother called him that. His nickname was short for tanner, the slang term for half a shilling – his brother was called Bob, which was slang for a shilling, and Tann was only half Bob's size. Another of my friends was called Jerry, who was an expert at climbing trees and catching baby birds, which he took from nests high in the treetops and raised himself. He had a jackdaw as one of his pets and it followed him everywhere. Our gang also included Martin and Phil, both from my class at grammar school, and together we maintained a deep respect for wildlife and nature.

In summer we would often play cricket together, while in winter we made icy slides on the fringes of the frozen lake and supped hot mugs of Ovaltine provided in the kitchens of benevolent mothers who lived in the elegant houses surrounding the lake. We were all lucky because none of us broke the ice and fell in, as adult warnings often predicted. In summer we built a raft and played out stories of adventures that we had heard read on *Children's Hour* on the wireless or that we had read in books about the Famous Five.

When we tired of the woods and the park we searched for pastures new in which to act out our adventurous fantasies. We moved over the road from Axwell Park to the banks of the River Derwent and played explorers as we paddled up river from Swalwell through woodland to the area around Winlaton Mill. One of our small party, Martin, had been given a canoe by his cousin who taught physical education and games in a senior school. This really opened up our opportunities for adventurous play. One day there were four of us in this long, open, wooden canoe. Two of us, one on either side, were paddling and pretending we were trailblazers on a mysterious river through hostile country. Suddenly we heard ahead of us the strident howling and baying of a dog. Navigating a bend in the turbulent river we came in sight of a small island of sand and gravel with sparse bushes growing on it. Marooned on this spit of land was a huge mongrel dog that was nervously pacing back and forth along the edge of the islet.

We attempted to rescue the animal by beaching the canoe and trying to entice the dog to come aboard with us. However, the current kept pushing the canoe around and once we almost capsized when we were standing up in our efforts to persuade the dog to join us. At last we gave up and paddled across to the opposite bankside where we were able successfully to moor the craft against the bank. We attached a rope from the front end of the canoe to a young tree. From there we witnessed the dog going crazier and crazier while stuck on the island.

His barks became so frenzied that I could bear it no longer. Stripping off my shirt, I waded into the river and swam the short distance to the gravel spit. Two of my friends followed me part of the way but stayed in the shallows ready to help. Thank goodness I had learned to swim properly when I went on holiday with my Uncle Fred and Aunt Betty. I easily reached the beach and the dog ran to me all friendly, wagging its tail and jumping up on me, wanting to be stroked. I patted and fondled him. He was young, little more than a puppy and he needed to be reassured that all was well.

Since the Derwent is a tidal tributary of the Tyne, its depth changes. I realized that the dog must have been able to cross over to the island through the shallows when the tide was low. Later, while he was busy sniffing around the bushes and boulder-strewn river debris, the river must have risen and when he encountered the fast current he must have lost his nerve and become too frightened to venture across. My coming comforted him and gave him confidence and so, grasping his collar, I led him to the river and pulled him in. Once he felt the waters around him he thrust out with me and soon we waded ashore, aided by my friends. The dog shook itself then raced off out of sight. What price gratitude?

It was a great experience for me and it raised my standing in the group. From then on I would often take the role of leader when we did things together.

It was blissful to feel a burgeoning independence, both inside and outside school now I had started at the grammar school. My health improved and I began to grow much stronger but it was chiefly my mind that was benefiting. I sensed a sort of liberation through contact with the world of arts and sciences. I felt that nothing could stop me now and I fell upon my books with a ravenous intellectual hunger.

A TERRIFYING DOG CALLED BRUNO

The backstreet culture of Mary Street, where we lived, was very diverse. Our neighbours may have been quite poor, but on the other side of the back lane the houses that fronted on to Blaydon Bank had conservatories and gardens. Some of the people who lived there were much better off than we were. At the top corner of the street lived Dr Morrison, whose large, wild garden provided a secret playground for myself and some of the other children in the street. Down from the doctor's house there lived a well-to-do family with a commercial business of some kind and next down was the house where Mr Markham had lived. Further down the lane most of the residents could often be seen at the front of their properties as their gardens overlooked the road. One house seemed more closed off, though – it was owned by a teacher, who worked at our school, and her sister, who seemed to be constantly sick.

Very few households had a car, which meant that transport was limited to either travelling by bus or walking. Returning from shopping expeditions laden with produce people tended to use the back-lane entry to their homes in preference to the front which required a longer walk. Bruno, a large mongrel dog, changed all that. He was the pet belonging to the teacher's sick sister and when he grew too big and lively to be kept indoors he started to spend most of his time outside. There he resided alone, without any attention for his need for proper exercise or to learn the skills of acceptable behaviour. After a brief reconnaissance Bruno decided that the street was ripe for take-over. To achieve this he positioned himself halfway up the cobbled strip in line with the residence of his owner. To all who dared now to venture up or down the lane this commanding position became known as 'Checkpoint Bruno'; it could not to be breached except at risk of personal injury.

Very few people dared to confront the ferocity of Bruno's warnings and several neighbours reckoned themselves fortunate not to have been bitten. If anyone deigned to ignore his barks Bruno would charge at them until they were chased away. Such was the alarming situation into which I walked late one afternoon on my return from school. Bruno and I came face-to-face for the first time. His first furious onslaught of barking and growls had no effect since I just stood in front of him completely dumbfounded at the belligerence of this dog in my backstreet.

'What do you think you are doing?' I said, keeping my voice as calm as I could.

Bruno, somewhat taken aback by my response, sat down and glared at me. Then he switched back into aggressive mode and charged at me until I was backed up against the wall at the side of the street. Having dealt with me he trotted off to resume his control point whilst I paused to review the situation. I was adamant on one point. I would not be domineered by a dog.

Having a quick think I recalled a story told by one of my father's brothers, Tony, a railway engineer who had lived and worked in South Africa while helping to establish the country's national railway system. One day when he was visiting the family, he came into my bedroom to chat to me and we sat by my room's small gas fire. He was a large man with big hands, a red face and thinning blond hair. He had undoubtedly summed me up accurately as something of a nervous, shy kid and I think he went out of his way to tell me a true story about a lioness in an attempt to toughen up my little-boy character. I remember looking at him and thinking that nothing on this earth would daunt this man who resembled, in the flesh, any one of my heroes from the pages of John Buchan's novels. The way he talked about his work brought Africa alive for me.

He told me that one day, while he was engaged in supervising the native work gangs building the South African railway, a lioness with two cubs approached their work camp and just sat and watched the activities. At the sight of the lions the workforce fled and hid in the bush yelling for my uncle and the two armed security guards to kill them. My uncle approached the lioness cautiously but noted that she showed no sign of aggression and simply sat up and watched as he drew near whilst the cubs prudently huddled against her side for protection.

'She was hungry,' my uncle said. 'With two growing cubs to feed she needed plenty of game and there wasn't so much available in that area. Besides which, lions are lazy animals and no doubt she could smell the cooking from the camp and was expecting to find some leftovers; perhaps she'd already benefited from other railway workings and was not afraid to take a chance on a free meal.'

What my Uncle Tony did next astounded his native gangs and showed the mettle of the man. 'I slowly walked towards her, holding the back of my left hand out facing her and without making eye contact, which can cause a fight response. I offered my hand to her face. She shifted her stance ever so slightly and then, as I'd expected, reached out with her enormous tongue and slavered all over my hand; she was just like a big dog.'

He then called the cook to bring whatever was left from the impala meat they had eaten the night before. Since the black African cook had a deep respect for the power of lions, he would not come very close, so my uncle gathered up the food and spread it out for the lions. 'To say that the lioness and her cubs relished the meal would be an understatement,' he continued. 'She followed our workings and visited us each morning as we pushed ever forward with the railway line. One morning, after about ten days, we looked out for her but she was gone and we never saw her or her cubs again. They had moved on, as we were doing, laying the rails and hacking a way through the bush.'

I remember his parting words to me: 'Let nothing daunt you. You can be and you can do whatever is necessary as long as you respect other living things but you need to believe in yourself first.'

As he said these words to me I reflected on how different my father was from some of his brothers. In his youth Uncle Tony had been a local champion snooker player, which wasn't the sort of thing I could imagine my father ever being. 'It's all a matter of knowing the angles, kid,' he said to me. 'Learn your geometry well and it will win snooker and billiard matches for you.'

Now the memory of my Uncle Tony's encounter with the lioness flashed through my mind as I faced the situation with Bruno. I decided in trepidation to try my uncle's ploy with the lioness. The big dog looked somewhat startled as I began slowly walking towards him and when several warning growls failed to deter me he resorted to loud barking, just the way bullies – of either the canine or human varieties – tend to do. I could tell from the bright yellow flecks showing in his eyes that he had expected me to run from his barking. Since I had now almost reached him he wasn't sure what to do.

Trying to control my fear I steadily began to extend the back of my left hand towards him. He watched my hand all the way to his muzzle and his eyes crossed in consternation and puzzlement. I stood firm although my heart was racing. Then, in a marvellous confirmation of my Uncle Tony's words, he reached out and licked my hand. My relief was palpable and I stroked his massive head and neck and spoke soft words to him. From that moment on he was mine. The big dog was getting what he had wanted all the time – affection and attention. By calling his bluff I had exposed his ordinary dog nature, the side that yearned for companionship and control.

He followed me to my back door and, when I turned to face him and ordered him to sit and wait, he didn't resist. He seemed willing to demure to my every command. It seemed like a miracle to me, although I expect it is something that all dog trainers know. I realized that Bruno had just been feeling lonely and neglected. He needed to be walked and given loving care and that is what I determined to give him as far as I could, although I did not dare take him into our house for obvious reasons. I hurried inside, deposited my school bag, filled my pocket with cornflakes and shouted hello to my mother who I could hear doing something upstairs.

Then, with Bruno following me, I called on his owner, a sickly looking young woman who stank of cigarettes. She responded enthusiastically to my request to exercise Bruno and gladly supplied me with a strong metal lead and a muzzle. She told me that since her husband was working away, Bruno had got out of control and she felt unable to do anything about it. I think she was one of the many people who acquire a lovable little puppy that grows into a dog that is far too large for them to control. Life can become a misery for everyone concerned, not least the dog. She warned me to be careful because he could be aggressive so I thanked her.

Once outside, watched by more than a few anxious neighbours, I attached Bruno's lead, causing him to start leaping for joy, and we set off together on our first walk, which I decided would be along the banks of the Tyne by the old racecourse. He was itching to be off and yet I detected in the way he walked to the lead a semblance of the discipline that someone had spent time schooling in him in the past, probably his lady-owner's husband who was no longer there for her or for Bruno.

As we got underway Bruno's eagerness for exercise consumed him and he began to tow me along the road as if I was in one of the Alaskan husky dog races I had seen on the big screen at the cinema. He was almost too much for me to restrain even though I shortened the lead and pulled him back to walk to heel. At last we reached the green pastures of the old racecourse, which was bordered by the clean upper waters of the River Tyne. Unable to curb his fervour any longer, I unclipped his lead from the body harness and told him, 'Go, boy, go.' He took off like the wind and was soon out of sight. It wasn't long before he came closer again, though, bounding his way towards me.

I walked in a sombre mood along the river banks, crunching my dry cornflakes. Haunting memories of a dog called Monty were heavy on my mind. Bruno, meanwhile, was busy pounding his way around me in ever decreasing circles until at last he collapsed at my side, with his tongue out and gasping for air. I had brought a small bottle of water with me and a large tin lid in anticipation of Bruno's needs. He noisily slaked his thirst with his newfound gusto for life. I felt sorry for his sickly owner, but I paused to think how misguided it was to leave a dog, and a big dog at that, stuck in a back lane with no other exercise than to harass passers-by. For the rest of the evening Bruno and I got along fine and, after an invigorating two hours of fresh air, we were both ready for home.

Bruno's owner thanked me on our return and I was glad to see that she had a large bowl of dog meat ready for him. After a hastily gulped meal of cold egg and chips which had been left out for me – my own fault for missing suppertime – I got stuck into my school homework, feeling on top of the world.

Whenever I could spare the time from school work I spent it with Bruno. We walked the hills, riverbanks and woods together and I showed him all my secret places. I took him walking on most evenings, weather permitting, and he was always likely to provide some excitement, especially if I unbuckled his lead for a while to allow him freedom to roam as I rested just to enjoy the view. Sometimes it was necessary to hasten to the aid of someone accosted by him. Even though I regularly fixed his muzzle when we were out together he could still present a formidable presence. Once, with his growls and fierce disposition, he cornered two terrified workmen who were taking a short cut home through the woods and I was called to the scene by their sounds of alarm. Sometimes in these situations, he would even snarl at me but usually my matter-of-fact attitude soon had him under control and once more attached to his lead.

He was great company and I soon realized what a bright and friendly dog he was. I ran errands for the neighbours to earn pocket money and, whether it was early morning or evening, I took Bruno with me. There was a dual purpose to this. Some of the older boys at my old school, St Joseph's Elementary School, would wander the backstreets looking for kids to rob and I had fallen prey to this in the past. But with Bruno at my side none of them dared to bother me. He proved to be a good friend and we shared many happy moments together as we divided a meat pie between us from the bakery shop or lay on our backs on a verdant hillside watching silver wisps of cloud chasing each other in the big blue sky.

Bruno, I realized, shared my own needs for love and attention and we were fortunate to have discovered each other. On one special evening, which I shall remember forever, I was resting on a slope of the riverbank, enfolded in the warm sunshine of a late summer evening. Bruno, meanwhile, spent an hour chasing black-headed gulls and huge gannets by crashing into the river over and again, simply for the fun of sending the birds shrieking and wheeling away from their feeding patches. The birds would then soar majestically over him, emitting their soulful cries that were so much the sound of the coast that lay just five miles downriver. When at last he finished his jollification he bounded back to where I was lying and shook himself all over me, drenching my T-shirt. It soon dried in the warm air and I didn't mind at all. The big dog was expressing his delight in being alive and free, just as we all need to do now and again.

I lay back against the grassy bank and breathed the flower scented air of eventide. I half-closed my eyes to better savour such a blissful moment. Slanting sunbeams charged the leaves of oak saplings behind me into a bouquet of rustic gold and Bruno, having finished rolling in the grass, came and lay on me. His face was directly in front of me and his eyes shone with flecks of green and yellow. Then this supposedly savage dog began to lick my face all over in a most caring way. According to dog lore he was paying me a compliment and giving me a treat. I submitted willingly enough and appreciated the sentiment, even though it felt awful. Afterwards we lay side by side in lazy repose and whiled the day away.

Good times are never everlasting and so it proved for me and Bruno. At school I was obliged to attend a residential environmental studies course at a centre far away in Northumberland for five days. When I returned there was no sign of Bruno at his back-lane station and in response to my enquiry I was informed, as I had begun to suspect, that he was gone. He had been put to death. His crime, I learned, was that he had bitten the leg of a man delivering coal who had dared to infringe his territory. Since there was no one to plead for a reprieve, capital punishment was immediately put into effect and Bruno was quickly gone forever. He remains just a fragment of my fond memories. I missed his dominant presence in our lane although others rejoiced at his going.

It was now autumn and one cold evening I retraced the route we had taken on a fine summer's day to lie in the sunshine by the River Tyne. The leaden, overcast skies were darkening when I approached the spot where that large, ferocious dog

126

had licked my face with tender loving care. There were wavelets on the river and the fierce wind blew sprinkles of spray that stung my face like icy needles. I already had tears in my eyes as I whispered a prayer for Bruno, who had proved to be too much for this world to accommodate. Saddened by a sense of loss I turned homewards knowing that life would never be quite the same on my country walks without the company of my big, rumbustious pal.

A BICYCLE AT LAST

I had passed the exam to go to grammar school and my twelfth birthday had come and gone, but I still hadn't managed to get a bike. My mother dithered about asking my father to get me one partly because she knew he would complain about the expense and partly because she was concerned about my safety – traffic on the roads seemed to be increasing every day and there were frequent reports of fatal road accidents in our area.

Eventually she asked him and wore him down until he at last conceded. One Saturday he took me to a shop in Blaydon High Street that sold shiny new bicycles. Entering the shop was a joyous moment for me. I had often lingered outside the shop, just staring at the window display of desirable machines. The prices were exorbitant but at last a basic 'sit up and beg' style bicycle was selected. It was a shiny black model with silver handlebars. A large deposit of my savings, with modest supplements from my Uncle John and my grandmother, was passed over the counter, and my father signed a form agreeing to pay the remaining three shillings and eleven pence each month for six months to complete the purchase. We were given a small blue book in which to record the payments and at last the deal was finalized. The bike would be available for collection on the following Monday.

Coming out of the shop I felt like I was walking on air. It was wonderful to think that come Monday I would at last have a bike of my own. My sense of mild celebration was not to last for long. Almost as soon as we had left the shop my father grabbed me roughly by the arm and snarled down at me.

'Make sure you get that money together because I'm not paying for it. You understand?' He then thrust the payment book into my hand and walked off.

I was shocked by his reaction and simply nodded. I realized once again what a mean and horrible man he was, totally different from the loving fathers of my friends, even those who came from homes more deprived than our own. If only I could have lived with the man I believed to be my true father, my Uncle Dan. Things would have been different and I would have had two brothers to support and play with me. My father never paid a penny towards my bike which I managed to pay for myself with a little help from my grandmother. In the meantime, he would thrust a written wager on the horse races into my hands, together with a ten shilling note, and say, 'Run along and give that to Bells the Bookie, and see you don't lose it.'

After I had collected it from the shop, my bike made up for many things that weren't right in my life. There were a few tools provided in a small leather bag that was attached behind the seat and it took me no time at all to make the necessary adjustments to the saddle and the pedals. I was soon able to mount my bike, thrust against the pedals and effortlessly glide away. I was ecstatic at having my own 'wheels' that finally gave me the freedom to go almost anywhere I liked, when I liked – it felt like I had been let out of prison. It was a momentous occasion in my life.

I cycled everywhere during the holidays. I could now do errands with greater speed and carry more shopping, strapping it on to the handlebars. I could now join up with my friends, all of whom already had bikes, and we could plan excursions. We would ride across to Rowlands Gill and Dunstan, and we often rode over Scotswood Bridge and cycled through Newburn and on to Prudhoe where we crossed the Tyne again. At this point we would stop by the green grassy banks of the river to eat our sandwiches and crisps. The waters by the upper reaches of the Tyne run crystal clear and we often plodged in the river shallows on sunny days and, removing our shirts, we splashed our faces and chests with the exuberant high spirits of boyhood. Then we mounted our bikes again and made our way down to Ryton and back to Blaydon. It was an exhilarating time to be a young teenage boy with a group of like-minded companions and to feel as free as the air we breathed.

Sometimes my friends would go out riding at night and to join them in these enterprises I needed to equip my bike with lights. Drawing on the extra money I had made by running errands by bicycle, I was able to buy a large lantern-like headlight to fix on to the front handlebars and a smaller, torpedo-shaped red light for the rear. Both of these lights needed batteries, which proved expensive. By emptying my money boxes I just about managed to afford it all. I was now set up, come rain or shine, to cycle around in both the day and the night. I felt truly independent, travelling all by myself without the need for buses or cars.

Then I had a lucky break. A boy who lived in the same street whom I knew only slightly told me that he was giving up his job of delivering newspapers for Hepples, the newsagent. He had seen me cycling around and was prepared to recommend me to the newsagent if I wished. I was overjoyed at the prospect and immediately went along with him to see the man in charge. Mr Long, as the shopkeeper was called, said he would give me a week's trial starting on Monday. Since it was now Thursday I arranged to meet up with my newfound friend early the next morning and do the delivery round with him to familiarize myself with the route. I was really excited at the prospect of having a regular job that would bring me some real pocket money. I was to be paid a shilling a day and half a crown (two shillings and sixpence) for Saturday and Sunday. My new bike had brought me good luck and prosperity as well as happiness.

My life now became much busier and so I did not welcome my father's demand that I should look after my sisters all day Saturday whilst he and my mother attended the horse races at Gosforth Park. I don't know where I summoned the courage from but I flatly refused to do it to his face. He became apoplectic. His face turned very red and I knew that in the next few moments he would start beating me until I agreed. I ran from the room, stopped to collect my bike and sped off.

I went to Mr Bramer's farm because I knew my father would never trace me there. The farmer and his wife seemed really pleased to see me although there was an air of sadness about the two of them that day.

'What's wrong?' I asked.

They told me that their daughter, who served with the Army as a typist and secretary, had been killed earlier in the year when a doodlebug, the nickname for Hitler's flying rocket bombs, had smashed into the government facility where she worked and exploded, killing everyone there. This coming weekend would have been a family celebration of her birthday. I sat with them in the big, old-fashioned kitchen as Mrs Bramer showed me photographs of their daughter, Jenny, when she was a child. Mrs Bramer softly cried as she passed around the photographs. After a while I made to leave but they would have nothing of it and insisted that I stay. I gathered that they needed someone young there to banish the haunting images of their daughter.

They asked me about my home and for a while I resisted telling them anything but in that emotionally charged atmosphere it eventually all tumbled out. They were angry at what had happened to me and at the behaviour of my father. Then, on a sudden impulse, Mrs Bramer said I could stay the night there and that I'd be doing them a favour to cheer them up. It was such a relief to be with such warm-hearted people that I didn't hesitate for a moment and agreed to stay the night with them. Besides, I loved being close to their animals. I knew that my father would be searching for me but once he realized that I wasn't at my grandmother's house he would not know where else to look. At least for tonight I'd be safe from his fury. I knew that my mother wouldn't worry too much as she would think I had gone to stay with one of my friends at Axwell Park, as I had done before.

The role of having to look after my sisters on Saturdays whilst my parents went to the dog racing at Gateshead or the horse racing at Hexham, Rothbury or Gosforth Park dated from when I was about nine or ten years old. My grandmother could not help because she worked on Saturdays and I think the old ladies who used to look after me had lost patience with babysitting so often for my parents. Since it was considered too dangerous to leave underage children alone in the house, we would be told to play in the street until their return. I would be threatened and bullied into taking responsibility for my sisters, including my sister, Gloria, who was young enough to still be in a pram. I'm not sure if my mother agreed to this practice, as I had often witnessed my father bullying her into attending functions with him.

I remember that several neighbours took exception to seeing three children – with two-year-old Gloria sometimes screaming her head off – having to wander aimlessly up and down the street in all kinds of weather. One Saturday someone called the police and they took us to a local home for children who had been orphaned in the bombing. Our parents were then arrested at the White City dog-racing track on Scotswood

Road. My parents were severely cautioned and threatened with the Magistrate's Court if the same thing happened again.

Despite this, my father had obviously decided that the time was ripe for him to get up to the same old trick again – perhaps he thought he could get away with it now I looked older. I always thought that his gambling was particularly despicable since he always kept my mother desperately short of cash for housekeeping. There was hardly ever enough food to feed the whole family. Food rationing was still in force and it was only through my grandmother being on such good terms with the butcher (they had gone to school together) that we sometimes had enough meat to feed us all. At meal times my father, as the working man of the house, always had to have the lion's share of the meat or suet pudding. Once, I remember watching him struggling so hard to swallow such huge portions of food that his eyes bulged just like a bloated frog.

I spent a most pleasant time at the farm. We had fresh ham, potatoes and garden peas, all produce of the farm. I ate until I couldn't eat any more. For dessert there were strawberries and clotted cream. There were no food restrictions here, only an abundance of healthy food provided by the sweat and toil of the farmer and his workers. We played dominoes on the gnarled oak table that dominated the vast kitchen, and were kept warm and cosy by the coke-burning Aga cooker. At bedtime I was shown up to a small attic bedroom at the top of the old farmhouse and given one of Mr Bramer's shirts to wear in bed. Crisp, white linen sheets enfolded me and I didn't wake until I heard the cockerel saluting the new morning. A huge symphony of birdsong joined the dawn chorus that soon stretched from one woodland to another. At its height it was a blast of sound, like massed choirs, receding to a melodic hymn to the daylight as the birds set about the serious business of finding food and feeding their young.

I was treated to a breakfast of bacon, two eggs, black and white pudding and homemade bread that had been fried in goose fat until crispy and then richly buttered. All this was washed down with steaming mugs of honey-sweetened hot tea stirred with fresh Jersey cream. It was beyond the dreams of a hungry young boy accustomed to wartime food shortages. I could hardly walk after such a delicious breakfast but helped out as much as I could by doing odd jobs around the farm. I fed the hens, took hay to Benny, the huge shire horse I'd first met in the hayfield, and mucked out his horse box.

I spent some time in the barn, letting my eyes become used to the gloom after the bright sun outside. After a while I could just make out the location of the swallow's nests, chiefly by watching the parent birds flying in with fresh batches of food. Judging from the size of the nestlings, I knew they would soon be leaving the nest. As they stared down at me from the edge of the nest, they looked so comically endearing that I couldn't help but laugh. The owls didn't make their presence known but I reckoned that they were probably in the darkest part of the barn waiting for rodents to appear below them.

I enjoyed helping out and seeing to the needs of the animals, and in the afternoon I joined Mr Bramer. He left most of the heavy work on the farm to George and Matthew, two farmhands who lived with their families in tied cottages on the site. Instead, he roamed the farm complex attending to all the minor things that needed fixing. He welcomed my company, and I was glad to keep him from dwelling too much on the death of his daughter.

Mr Bramer kept up a rambling commentary as we meandered through the farm enclosures.

'That's where a goshawk took my cockerel and virtually wiped out my poultry one year and yonder is where a pine marten broke into a shed and killed half a dozen geese I was keeping for the Christmas Market one year.'

Then, as if he'd had a sudden thought that was irresistible, he led me off the beaten track to a heavily barricaded compound.

'Come and meet Mogolan,' he said.

He opened a door to a corridor that led up to a gate with an iron-barred window.

'Take a look through there,' he said, smiling.

At first I couldn't see anything and then a massive, light-coloured form moved and a colossal head turned towards me.

'It beats me how those Spanish fellows – what do you call 'em? – can face one of those and take it on.'

His words broke my trance as I stared at the most terrifying animal I had ever seen. It was a giant bull bristling with latent power and full of incipient fury and aggression. I stared at

Mogolan in petrified silence and the bull, through cold, hostile, pebble eyes rimmed with red, stared back at me.

'Would he hurt you?' I asked naively.

'He would kill me without a moment's notice and he'd relish doing it.' I shivered despite the warmth in the air. 'But he wasn't always like that. You see that bull there, he's a prize animal, worth thousands of pounds, but all he can put his mind to just now is blind lust, how to get to and mate with the cows he knows are somewhere around here. He can scent them and anything and everything that gets in his way, stopping him from doing that, must be smashed.'

Mr Bramer went on to tell me about a cold windy night in March two years earlier when his best cow gave birth in the early morning to Mogolan, a robust, cream-coloured little bull. He was everything the Bramers had hoped for and he had the sweetest temperament of any animal they had ever known.

'He followed us round like a dog,' said Mr Bramer. 'If I whistled and called for him he'd come running and he would allow us to pet and fondle him as much as we wanted and he took treats from our hands.'

'So what changed things?' I asked.

'Sex. That's what changed him. He got full of testosterone, that's the male hormone that drives male animals to mate with the females but in horned beasts it brings on what is called the "Rutting Madness". That's what changed him. Anything and anybody that isn't a female in receptive heat is a mortal enemy. I had hoped that there'd still be something left of the affection we had for each other but there's nothing there now. One day earlier this year I went into his pen to give him a rub down and he charged me, put me down and kept butting my chest. Somehow I managed to roll out from under him and George came in just then and fended him off me until I could climb out the pen. He'd have killed me for sure, there and then.'

Mr Bramer laid a fatherly hand on my shoulder and warned me, 'Never get between a cow and her calf and never get near a bull in rut and that goes for stags as well. Sometimes even a ewe with lambs will attack you and a full grown ram is always dangerous.'

Such were the lessons I learned in an afternoon from this unassuming, kindly man. The experience with Mogolan made me think that there were animals in the world that, despite every effort, would not be responsive to love and caring.

The Bramers prevailed upon me to stay a further night, an invitation that I was more than happy to accept.

'Has he been filling you with farm talk to frighten you?' Mrs Bramer asked as we sat down to dinner.

'No,' I replied. 'I've learned more in an afternoon than in six months at school.'

'Well, I never did hold much value on schooling,' she said. 'My mother taught me to read and the rest that's worth knowing I've learned right here.'

We spent another carefree, pleasant evening together and in the morning, after another perfect night's sleep, I prepared to return home. First, I decided, I would check what my grandmother was doing. As I was about to leave Mr Bramer brought out a bag filled with food.

'Just a little something from the missus and me to feed a growing lad and make him strong,' he said. 'Come back and stay with us again soon.'

I promised that I would. I hugged them both in turn and then cycled away with the heavy bag swinging from the handlebars.

My grandmother wasn't in when I got to her place but I was able to get inside by putting my hand through the letterbox and grabbing the key hanging from a string behind the door. She was amazed when she came in to see the food I had set out on the table. Mr and Mrs Bramer had given me a dozen eggs, a large ham, some sausages and a plucked chicken. I told her all about the people at the farm and how kind they were and that I had stayed there the last two nights. My grandmother was overwhelmed by their largesse and said that they must be exceptional people. She then stored away the food, saying that she'd take some up to my mother the following day.

She told me the news I had been waiting to hear: my father had rampaged around looking for me and threatening blue murder. My grandmother said that she would speak to my mother about leaving the children alone while to they went out gambling.

'It's not right,' she said with a stern face. 'It's not seemly.'

I told her that I would be back later and cycled to the lake at Axwell Park. I had hoped to meet up with some of my friends but, as none of them was there, I simply rode up to the far corner of a field to think through my present troubles. Sitting under a tree by the lake, my heart was soon filled with calmness as I began to tune in to the harmony surrounding me. I could hear a great spotted woodpecker hammering the bark of a silver birch to uncover insects and a pair of red squirrels was chittering away in the higher branches of a horse chestnut. There were no alarms or cries of fear. Nothing alerted anything else to the possibility of danger because, in this little pocket of time, there was none. This small enclave seemed to be clothed in a spell of profound peace. It would not last forever but whilst it did, it offered a kind of medicine to those willing to embrace it. I closed my eyes and felt renewed. I would be able deal with whatever was coming my way once I had returned home.

I cycled homewards intending to spend as little time as possible there. The family were just sitting down to supper and my mother ushered me to my place at the table.

My father glared across the table at me and demanded, 'And where do you think you have been?'

'I've been staying with my friends,' I replied not meeting his gaze.

He started to say something else but my mother called for hush at the table.

'I'll see you later,' he said.

He didn't get the chance. As soon as I had finished eating I said, 'Bye, Mum,' and left the kitchen while he was still struggling to rise from his seat. I grabbed my bike and rode down to my grandmother's house with a light heart as the evening sunshine projected the shadow of me and the bike, prancing ahead of me. I stayed the night at my grandmother's house and next morning I cycled down to the River Derwent at Swalwell. I was determined to make the most of the remaining time of the school summer holidays.

I slowed up my cycle ride to take in the colours of the late summer as it drifted into autumn, my favourite time of the year. The low morning sun caught the mist on the river and shone through the reeds lining the river bank, lighting a red fire behind them. Filled with the uncompromising possessiveness of early adolescence, I thought such scenes were mine alone to keep and savour. If others came to disturb the solitude of these moments, I would slide away unseen – like the partridge and the doe, I knew how to hide.

I felt myself maturing, shedding some of the childhood nature of waiting, powerless, for things to happen. I had become a little more assured now that my life had started moving in the direction I desired. Sometimes I found it enormously difficult to stop thinking about the river, the lake and the woods, and would leave images of them secretly couched at the back of my mind even while doing something else. Other things now needed my attention as much as possible, as I began in earnest to concentrate on my grammar-school career.

THE FINAL BEATING

Dressed smartly, with a resplendent school badge adorning the new blazer my mother had bought for me, I felt the impending weight of my initiation into the new chapter of my life. It was my first day at Blaydon Grammar School, but strangely it was to bring the ghosts of the past to face me yet again. My first class was interrupted by a message from the school secretary that the headmaster, Mr Locket, wished to see Denis O'Connor. My mind swiftly moved from a happy-go-lucky mode into an anxiety state because, in my previous school, to be sent for by the headmaster meant trouble and usually punishment. And so it was with mounting trepidation that I approached Mr Locket's door and nervously knocked.

'Come in,' a voice barked from within the sanctum.

I entered a large office, which smelt of leather and was lined with books all around the walls. Before me stood Mr J. Locket swathed in a black academic gown. I was overwhelmed. He coughed twice to clear his throat and to indicate the serious nature of what he was about to say.

'Well, O'Connor – Denis O'Connor – I hope that you will make the most of your time here with us.' This was followed by another two coughs. 'But I need to tell you, in fact to warn you, that your Uncle Dan was a pupil here and although he did very well he caused a great deal of trouble for me and the other teachers by his difficult behaviour.'

Mr Locket coughed yet again and this time I could smell the odour of cigarettes coming from him. I was beginning to wonder what on earth my Uncle Dan had done, and what this had to do with me on my first day at grammar school.

Mr Locket drew himself up, coughed once more, and with a slightly embarrassed tone to his voice said, 'And so I want to warn you that I won't stand for any nonsense or there'll be trouble.'

His words seemed to hang in the air as if awaiting some kind of confirmation. When he sat down behind his desk, finally I realized that he had finished and was waiting for me to go. I turned and left the room in an utterly bemused state of mind and returned to my class. I felt that I had been accorded the status of a rebel-in-waiting, but only the future would tell if this label had any substance.

Later during my time at grammar school I looked upon this incident as not only amusing but as prophetic. I believe that, eventually, there was a basic level of respect, touched with affection, in the relationship between us, but on many occasions Mr Locket would become exasperated and sometimes downright dumbfounded at the kind of things that I got up to during my time under his care. There were quite a few incidents that must have caused him headaches and frustration.

I remember that when I was in the fourth form I announced that I no longer wished to play football or rugby, as they had no appeal for me, and that I preferred to play cricket, which I had enjoyed playing throughout the summer with my new friends in Axwell Park. I remember seeing Mr Locket charging down to the cricket nets where a few friends and I were spending the games period. Looking straight at me, as he had rightly assumed that I was the ring leader in this plan of action, he informed us that we must cooperate with the games master and play other ball games. I politely informed him – having just become acquainted with Plato's commentaries on Socrates – that my decision was final and not open to negotiation because it was based on reason rather than momentary impulse. After a heated exchange he withdrew and left us alone.

The games master also remonstrated with us but I remained adamant and eventually he capitulated when all five of us declared that we were practising so that we could at some later time play for England. The farcical arrogance of this statement left him flabbergasted. But the really crazy aspect of this incident was that at the time, inspired by the radio commentaries on the Ashes series between England and Australia, we really believed what we said. It was a case of adolescence at its worst and I believe that the headmaster and the sports teacher decided to just let it work itself out. We reached a compromise which I believed was a truly demo-cratic outcome. During games periods we would practise batting and bowling at the nets, but when the weather was inclement then we would practise the other cricketing skills: slip-catching, fielding, running wearing leg pads, repairing equipment and so on. There were other times when my many misdemeanours were shrugged off by the headmaster, who turned out to be a truly understanding educationist who was at heart a benign supporter of youthful development.

Since I had started grammar school, life at home had taken on a new routine in which I spent less time face-to-face with my father. There was a great deal of homework to be tackled each night and even more at weekends. To begin with, I also spent time walking and training Bruno, so I found myself very busy indeed. Then there was the extra time I liked to spend at my grandmother's house where I did supplementary reading of the classics from my Uncle John's library.

Grammar-school life also created a new cultural dimension for me because it was a co-educational school. With the opposite sex around all the time, I had a new raft of interests and concerns. There were frequent parties to attend as well as school dances, which were designed to broaden the scope of the educational experience. Inevitably there were pairings off and, when I turned fourteen, I found a soulmate in Nancy. She lived with her parents and a younger sister in a well-to-do part of Dunston, a former village which had become a suburb of Gateshead. When lessons were over we tended to spend time in the school library doing some of our homework. As we became better acquainted we sometimes met up to go for walks together and one weekend we went to a late showing at the Plaza Cinema. As we emerged from the cinema I was hailed in friendly fashion by a workmate of my father. I didn't

think much of the incident at the time nor of the dire conse-
quences I would have to face because of it.

On the following Monday evening I was working at my
school books on the table in the small sitting-room adjoining
the kitchen when my father came home from work. I heard
him tersely ask my mother if I was in and then he charged
into the sitting-room. He smelled of sawdust and wood resin,
and he was still dressed in his work overalls. His face was
already swollen red with aggression when he confronted me.

'Is it true?' his voice blasted at me. 'Are you courting a girl
from that Protestant dump of a school you are at?'

I stood up quaking at his manner and replied that I had
gone to the pictures with a girlfriend from my class but that I
wouldn't call it courting. It was simply a normal friendship,
and lots of my friends in the class did the same.

He slammed the back of his hand into my face with such
force that it broke my nose and lacerated my cheek and lips as
his ring cut into my skin. I fell to my knees as he rained blows
to my head, which made me reel about the floor as stars really
did flash before my eyes and a zinging started in my ears. Next
he began kicking me with his heavy workboots and I began
retching. I suddenly believed that he intended to beat me to
death. I felt a terrible pain in my ribs as he continued the
onslaught. He kept on shouting during the attack, calling me
'a Godless damned whelp who should never have been born'.
But it was his eyes that I remember most. As I looked up at
him through the blood running down my cheeks I saw the

eyes of a maniac who believed that I was beyond the redemption and mercy of his all-powerful God.

All at once there was a tigress standing over me as my mother positioned herself between my father and me. She screamed and shrieked at him like she was possessed with a fiendish spitting fury and he stopped kicking me, surprised by the venom in her voice and the look in her eyes. Lying on the floor with blood still streaming down my face, I half raised myself up and watched him as he slunk away. I swear that I could perceive wisps of sinister black vapour coiling around the lower parts of his body – perhaps it was the resin impregnated in his clothes turning into steam with the heat of his exertions. Then I passed out.

When I awoke I was being bandaged by friendly old Dr Morrison, whom I heard explaining to my mother that such episodes were best kept within the family and it would be preferential if the boy could spend some time with a relative until most of the healing was done.

'Meanwhile,' he said, 'I will have a word with your husband.'

He would also sign a sick note to cover my absence from school since it was best that I rest up for a while. He would call on me again when he knew where I was residing.

And so I was taken once more to the loving home of my grandmother. I could barely walk because of the bruising to my legs and ribs, so moving me from my parent's house proved something of a problem. In the end, my mother and grandmother managed to arrange me sitting sideways in a Silver

Cross pram, which had been used for my sisters when they were babies, with my legs hanging over the side. It was lucky that I was small and slight for my age. After dark, so that the neighbours wouldn't see, I was then wheeled to my grandmother's house.

My grandmother was enraged about the extent of the battering my father had given me and wanted to call in the police. After due consideration and counselling from the local Justice of the Peace, it was decided not to proceed on this course because if my father was imprisoned the family would have no income. Such was the state of affairs in 1948, when the country was still in a severely impoverished state following the Second World War. My mother called in at church and told the new parish priest, Father Kennedy, who simply reminded her that her duty in marriage was to be a good wife to her husband. As for me, the priest said that parents had an obligation to guide their children away from the temptations of sin. When I heard this I had a fearful feeling that my father could do whatever he liked to me and I was powerless to escape his temper. However, the priest did talk to my father about his behaviour.

I wrote to Nancy giving her only the briefest details of my 'accident' and asking her to save her lesson notes for me to copy when I got back to school. The following weekend, on the Saturday morning, Nancy came to my grandmother's house asking if she could see me. When she was shown in and saw me lying on the sofa, still covered with bruises and bandages, she began to cry. We had tea and my grandmother's cupcakes and she promised to call back the following week to share her notes with me. I asked her not to say anything to anybody but the news of my condition was soon circulating throughout the school. I first became aware of this when I began receiving a number of sympathy cards.

Nancy was sent for by a senior female teacher and asked in confidence what precisely had happened to me. The teacher then told Mr Locket who in turn questioned Dr Morrison, who also happened to be the school doctor. To my great surprise, Mr Locket visited my grandmother's house and expressed great concern for my condition, saying that, as I was a pupil at his school, he had an official responsibility to look after my care. He told me that I would be welcome back at school as soon as I could walk and that every effort would be made to keep me up to date with my studies. He then insisted on going to see my father back at home.

In the days following I was able to cobble together the gist of this meeting. Mr Locket was already well aware of my father's violent family background as some of the O'Connor brothers had a reputation for getting involved in fights with other men in the town. Mr Locket threatened to have me taken into fostering care under the auspices of Durham Education Authority, which would consider very seriously a recommendation from the school. After talking to my grandmother, Mr Locket decided not to initiate this course at the present juncture but he let my father know that he would not hesitate to proceed if circumstances warranted it in the future. I felt uplifted to receive such support and soon began to feel better because of it. It was good to know that others were aware of the way I was treated and were prepared to do something about it.

Soon I was able to return to school and was well received by my classmates. My studies picked up at pace and in the end of term examinations I came top of the class in Maths and was awarded the prize of 7 shillings and 6 pence in National Savings Stamps. My mother and grandmother were over the moon at my success but my father simply growled that 'the rest of the class can't be up to much then'.

As it turned out, he never beat me again although I always sensed his hatred for me whenever I was near him.

Sometimes I found the reality of my father's hatred too much to bear emotionally. Even if I wasn't his child then surely the fault lay elsewhere. It made no sense to me at all and I found myself at times still struggling against all the odds to win some approval, if not affection, from him. But it never worked. Life can be cruel but to be hated for who you are rather than what you have done is enough to cripple the spirit of any person. He hated me for the rest of his life, but it was particularly damaging during my childhood years.

His inclinations to attack me physically may have been mollified somewhat by the counselling of the good Dr Morrison and the parish priest, not to mention the warning from Mr Locket, but his treatment of me did not improve. In place of his fist, his interactions with me now were filled with toxic mockery, both in front of members of my family or when strangers were present. When people appeared to be amused by his comments, particularly if anyone sniggered or laughed aloud, he would smile broadly as if he had scored an important point. He helped divide people's opinions of me: some people assumed that I was worthy of his contempt and shared it without questioning the reasons that lay behind it, while others saw that it was wrong. Inevitably, there was friction with those he turned against me – which included my sisters, family members and other people whom I had previously regarded as friendly. As a result, I tended to withdraw into the persona of a hard-working student with little or no interest in what was going on at home.

In fact, I had another secret outlet for my interests and imagination that my father could not sully. During the war, after he had been called up to serve in the Navy, my mother took a job as a cashier at the Pavilion Cinema. As my mother worked there I could get in free, with the approval of the manager, to see any film I wanted. I had a keen interest in all things to do with film so I soon befriended the operators of the massive machines in the projection room. They let me help out and showed me how to rewind the huge reels of film and how to repair them if the film snapped. After the war ended my mother continued to work in the cinema for a while, despite the protests of my father. The appeal of the extra money and newly gained sense of independence was irresistible for her. During her time there I continued to have access, as soon as my homework was done, to most of the major films of the 1940s and early 1950s. I would sit there and just lose myself in another world, free from the taunts and jibes of my father.

ATTACK AT THE STABLES

I have always loved horses or, more exactly, I have always loved the idea of horses. From my earliest sight of a cowboy riding a horse in the Saturday morning cinema shows for children I have been obsessed with horses and longed for the day when I might be able to ride one. In conversation with some of my classmates I learned about a riding school called High Meadows, which was situated near the hospital where I had been taken after the death of my dog Monty. I was told that the owners of the riding school welcomed youngsters to help muck out the stables and assist in the general grooming of the horses. This was where I first met Wildfire, a seven-year-old mare, sometime later. She was a horse of many colours, whose kind the cowboys always referred to as a 'pinto' or paint horse, which was favoured by Native Americans, especially the Comanche tribe. She had a dark brown face, a white neck and mane, and was covered in large brown, white and black patches over the rest of her body. Her true equine description is that she was a 'skewbald', which is similar to a piebald, but they only have black and white colouring. She was a fine-looking horse and later was to play a significant part in my life.

Before I got to know Wildfire, the stables (as the riding school was always known) gladly accepted me as a volunteer and I became a regular helper on Saturday and Sunday mornings. My enthusiasm and obvious regard for the horses had been noted and occasionally I was offered a small payment for my services. Every now and again I was also given a free ride and after a time I managed to become a proficient rider. Luckily, I took to it very quickly and, after a couple of years, I was allowed to lead a group of paying novices. I was paid a little bit of money for what I regarded as a privilege, and sometimes the older riders would give me a tip for my services. I never felt free to mention this at home because I knew that it would only invite more taunting. Later, when I started riding more regularly at the stables, I did tell my mother but asked her not to tell anyone else.

One day during a half-term holiday I was busy at the stables helping to prepare the horses for a group riding session. By then, I not only held these animals in high esteem but felt a kind of love for them. I admired the high degree of sensitivity they showed to people and other horses, and liked the life-force within them that made them want to run for the utter joy of it. If you give a horse love, it often gives you love back – like cats and dogs, they are the sort of animals that need to be loved and cared for to be at their best. I had also soon come to realize that it was important to develop a healthy respect for these large animals, which can weigh up to half a ton.

On this day, one of the riders was a doctor's wife who had gone to great lengths to look the part of a horsewoman: she wore all the traditional gear, including shiny, long black boots, white jodhpurs, a white blouse and a dark jacket, all surmounted by a black bowler hat. She also wore a white silk scarf around her neck, which was constantly catching in the wind and blowing this way and that – horses are quite nervous creatures and something like that is a sure way to unsettle them. Her mount that day was a mare called Honey, a beautiful chestnut standing at seventeen hands.

As I led Honey towards the rider I could detect the alarm beginning to surface in Honey's eyes as the scarf continued to waft about all over the place. She started snorting, throwing her head about and generally acting alarmed. I thought she would soon calm down, but after the lady had mounted I began to sense the real possibility of danger. A stable girl was calmly attempting to fit the lady's boot into the stirrup, while the unsettled Honey moved about. The lady was becoming increasingly frustrated with the situation and now acted with outstanding lack of insight. She decided to blame the horse for her predicament and, raising her riding crop, gave Honey a sharp whip across the rump. The horse had endured enough. She had experienced apprehension, as all riding-school horses do, at who might be her mount for today. Then she had been startled at being confronted by the sight of the doctor's wife dressed in her formal hunt riding attire, with her scarf flashing about. This was followed by the lady in question seeking to mount her in the most clumsy manner possible and to end it all she had been whipped.

This was beyond endurance and she did what most horses naturally do at this point. She ran as fast as she could, dumping the good lady on her backside among all the muck of the stable yard. As I was standing nearby, I tried to grab Honey's loose reins as she made off. Sensing that an attempt was being made to stop her, Honey lashed out with her rear legs. It nearly always seems to be an innocent bystander who suffers most in accidents. One of Honey's flailing hooves kicked me hard in the left thigh just below my groin. The force was tremendous and I was knocked flying. I lay heavily on my back, feeling stunned and semi-paralysed. Within seconds I was suffering waves of nausea and pain, and felt sure that I was about to be sick.

Some people standing around thought that it was only a half-hearted kick, but I was knocked for six. I had to be helped to the barn where I lay among the hay waiting for the effects to wear off. Two of the stable girls came to where I was resting to ask me how I was and if I was thinking of attending the evening musical festival to be held in Alnwick. I replied that I desperately needed a lift home because, far from being able to dance, I couldn't even walk. One of the older hands at the stables had a van and kindly gave me a lift home to my grandmother's house. I spent the next two days recuperating. I was left with a massive black and purple bruise on my leg but I was most thankful that the kick had not been any higher.

I soon returned to limp around the stables to see if I could be of any use on days that I was free. I found that my attention was increasingly drawn to a quiet, solitary horse in one of the small side paddocks.

When I asked Vera, who jointly owned the stables, about the horse, she rapidly fired off some details: 'She's a mare belonging to local lad called Anthony who dabbles in horse breeding. He has a chestnut stallion he keeps down in a field adjoining the Duke's Park. She's called "Wildfire" with the accent on the "Wild". We've tried to use her here on our escorted rides but she's awkward and difficult to control. I think she's just stupid and lazy.'

'Is she rideable?' I asked tentatively.

'We've tried her a few times but she's too much for our novices,' declared Vera. 'She wouldn't fit in here.'

In her eyes, it seemed that Wildfire was unfit-for-purpose and this explained why the multicoloured horse was in solitary confinement in the far paddock. I stumbled and limped my way up to Wildfire's paddock to introduce myself. As I approached, she was busy grazing but lifted and shook her magnificent head, which was adorned by a long white mane that looked like silk as it billowed in the air. She observed me with careful scrutiny. We studied each other in silence for a while but I was at a loss for what to say. Eventually I ventured an opening: 'You're not stupid, are you?'

Upon hearing my voice she nodded her head and gave a soft, throaty whinny. I think we both sensed a coming together of soulmates.

Anthony, her owner, worked as a milkman as well as horse breeder and proved difficult to track down. He was something of an entrepreneur and had many jobs, sometimes working in the timber yards at the sawmill and at one time he owned a small fishing boat. A tall, well-built man, he could be very genial. Anthony, I gathered from people's comments about him, had also experienced a difficult childhood since his parents were strict Plymouth Brethren. He had left home in his early teens and from then on had become estranged from his family. Eventually I managed to contact him and talked about Wildfire. The outcome of our discussion was that I could ride the horse whenever I had time enough. He appreciated that it would be good if the horse could get more regular exercise.

'Get one of the stable girls to help you to harness and bridle her and there's a saddle in the shed in the corner of the paddock,' he said as he fished a grubby key out of his similarly grubby jeans. He handed the key to me. 'She's a fine horse but not easy to control. Don't ever hit her. There are other ways to win her confidence and she's been whipped too much in the past.'

And with that he was off – he had proved to be courteous but not a charmer, rather like his horse.

I went to see Wildfire as often as I could and regularly took her carrots and apples that the green grocers put out as waste in the lane behind the Co-operative store. I recall the day I first touched her. I wouldn't call her a nervous horse – she was

160

just wary. Whenever I got what she considered to be too close she moved away and faced me head-on; the look in her eyes was apprehensive and vigilant. This action brought to my mind Anthony's comment, 'Don't ever hit her.' Anthony had also mentioned that at an early age Wildfire had been trained as a steeplechase horse but that he knew nothing further. This gave me cause for concern because I'd once heard my Uncle Chris, one of my father's older brothers, say that when he'd been training as a stable lad some of the jockeys would give an obstinate and unresponsive horse a real 'going over', which entailed punching and slapping them. If this had happened to Wildfire then it would explain her awkward behaviour and her extreme wariness whenever people came too near to her. This horse had been badly hurt in the past and I gave a little shiver as I empathized with her.

Whenever I could steal the time away from homework and running errands I would go and talk to her when no one else was around. Horses are extremely sensitive animals; they are certainly not stupid. In the short time I had spent with Wildfire I had become impressed with her as a fine horse capable of much more than spending her time in lonely isolation. I determined that, at the weekend, I would saddle her up and ride her if I could.

That Friday heralded the beginning of the summer holidays. On Saturday morning I got up good and early. After making myself a hearty, uplifting mug of tea, mixed with local raw honey, and a jam sandwich I set off to keep an appointment with Wildfire. Arriving at her paddock I was astonished to find it strewn with clumps of soil, pieces of wood and stones. I discovered Wildfire standing behind the shed in which her tackle was stored. She was bleeding from several small gashes to her rump and flanks.

Just then Amanda, who co-owned the stables with Vera, arrived and parked her vehicle at the back of the stables. She looked over the fence and exclaimed, 'So they've been at it again have they? Is she hurt?'

'Yes,' I replied. 'Who are "they"?'

In the meantime, other members of the stables' staff arrived and amongst the general natter and clatter my question seemed to have got lost, so I repeated it again. It was Vera who answered.

'"They" refers to the rabble of youngsters who amuse themselves by hurling missiles, whatever they can find, at dumb animals.'

Then Vera began instructing another girl to phone the vet and the police, in that order.

'It's a good job we can lock the stables,' somebody else said.

There was a general air of commotion around the place, which was quite unusual for the weekend. The horses needed watering and feeding, and there were several rides booked that morning. My plan of work with Wildfire obviously had to be aborted as my services were required elsewhere. As we all busied ourselves with the work that needed to be done, there was still much concern about what seemed to be the perennial problem of attacks on the animals that were left outside in fields with inadequate fencing. Horses in particular seemed to be most at risk from the thugs and there were examples of the most diabolical cruelty perpetrated against them.

It transpired that the injuries to Wildfire were only superficial, which did not rule out the emotional damage that had been done to a horse that had already suffered hardship. It was all very upsetting to contemplate and now extra care would have to be taken to defend the animals from such attacks in the future. Whatever the security measures, it seems that there are always people who are prepared to go to great lengths to inflict pain on defenceless animals. In any case, repair men were called in to make the fences higher and more impregnable, and life at the stables settled down once more.

As the holidays progressed, I had the time to really get to know and befriend Wildfire, whom I was still hoping to ride. The next time I went to the stables, I picked up a bridle, blanket and saddle and found her grazing in the top corner of her newly reinforced paddock. I put the riding gear down behind me to make sure that I didn't alarm her. She saw me and, recognizing me as the boy with the carrots, she trotted over and whickered a hello. I have always, since I was a young child, believed that animals should be talked to, despite how odd this might seem to some people. The interesting outcome of this is that they appear to understand and respond to the attention they gain from such conversing. I started to chat to Wildfire.

'Hello,' I said. 'I've been thinking a lot about you and I'm so sorry about what happened to you the other night. We're all going to see that it doesn't happen again. Anyway I didn't like some of the things people have been saying about you, didn't like them at all.'

Having eaten her way through a small pile of carrots I'd given her, Wildfire started nodding her head and making affectionate horse noises in her throat.

'Well,' I continued, looking straight at her, 'I don't think that you are stupid at all and further, I don't think that you are obstinate and lazy and I'm going to give you the chance to get together with me to prove it.'

With that said I picked up the bridle from the ground where I'd placed it behind me. While offering her a small carrot near the tongue piece of the bridle, I fitted her with it, which she accepted quite placidly. For the present I let the reins dangle down and, picking up the blanket, I placed it over her back. She never really moved at this manoeuvre but simply readied her back by straightening up a little. I guessed she was already anticipating the saddle. Soon I was tightening her saddle strap, especially around her stomach. She tried to fool me, as horses do, by bloating her stomach out but she did not object when I pulled the strap secure. Looping the reins over her head I was now ready to mount her. Springing up into the saddle I felt comfortable and just right.

Wildfire turned her head to look at me as if to say, 'Whenever you are ready.'

And with that we were off on a walking tour of the stables and the nearby training field. We made a couple of circuits and at one point she broke into something of a joyous canter. I headed back to the paddock, unsaddled her, gave her a rub down and some horse nuts, and, after much stroking and patting, told her several times that she was a good horse.

My ride on Wildfire had been noted by other workers at the stables. It wasn't long before a number of the girls, who showed love for every single one of the horses, were anxious to try her out for a ride and were delighted with the outcome. Wildfire was becoming popular and I was given the credit for her rehabilitation. Fortunately for me, there were days when she was still all mine and we rode with the freedom that humans and horses have shared for thousands of years.

I felt especially privileged as a boy of fourteen years to have what amounted to virtually my own horse to ride. Throughout my childhood I had developed an attachment to the myths and legends of the Wild West. I was able to play out my fantasies of riding through the land of the pioneering cowboys whilst venturing alone along woodland trails and over patches of moorland. I would act the role of a lone cowboy searching the landscape for stray cattle and rustlers whilst ever watchful for Comanche war parties.

With mature hindsight I realized that my experiences at the stables, particularly with Wildfire, helped me to counterbalance the distress I was still suffering at home. She gave me the chance to give and receive an uncomplicated love, free from the restrictions that tainted my home life. Animals had become my surrogate family. The love which I had received from my dog Monty, from big Bruno and from Wildfire was an antidote to the poisonous feelings extended to me from my father. Their presence made my life more palatable and enabled me to lay the foundations of self esteem that I would need to carry me through life's enigmas.

WILDFIRE

The summer of 1948, which followed one of the harshest winters, was not especially warm but I wanted to enjoy being outdoors to the full, and in early August I had a clever idea. First, I needed the permission of Anthony, which he readily gave, and then I needed the support of the stables management as they were the caretakers for Anthony's horse, and they granted me permission, too. Now I felt that I could go ahead and consult my grandmother. I was over the moon when she proved most supportive as well, but she cautioned me against the risks involved.

The idea was this. I would go camping on horseback for a few days in the Derwent Valley and perhaps on the moors over towards Stanhope. I lost no time in planning this adventure. Using my earnings at the stables, I was able to buy a small RAF tent and some of the other things I needed for the trip from the Army and Navy Store in Newcastle. My friends at Axwell Park, most of whom were classmates of mine at the grammar school, were most enthusiastic about my proposed adventure. They promised to visit my camp to bring me supplies and perhaps join me for a night around the campfire. I may have been young, but I realized that the trip was unlikely to turn out as romantically as I had first envisaged.

Nevertheless, this in no way reduced my determination to complete all the practical preparations and to have a jolly good time with Wildfire, my four-legged friend.

To my mind, the Derwent Valley was the best possible place for such an adventure. The name Derwent may derive from the Celtic and means River of Shining or the Smiling River – either definition seemed right to me as I had already spent many happy summer hours with my friends enjoying its waters. The old word 'Derwentian' provides another definition: the river abounding in oaks. In 1892, W. J. Palmer wrote that the valley was so densely wooded that a red squirrel could travel from Axwell Park to Shotley Bridge, ten to twelve miles distant, without once touching the ground. Although the mass of woodland had receded since Palmer's day, the area was still extensively forested.

I had made a swift reconnaissance by bicycle of where to make my initial camp and decided on a strip of land that protruded out into the river and was backed by a sheer rockface. I gathered twigs and dried moss as kindling and called over to the stables to collect the horse nuts and grain to feed Wildfire, who would also be able to graze along the way. I had decided to start off on Monday to avoid meeting up with too many walkers and hikers who tended to use the area mostly at weekends.

On the Saturday before I was due to set off, Anthony made a surprise call at my grandmother's house to advise me on how best to manage the horse when I was out trekking.

'Don't overdo the first day,' he told me, 'as both the horse and yourself will be extra tired the next day. And remember to stop and water the horse at least every hour.'

He gave me some salt pellets in case Wildfire sweated a lot and a horse blanket in case the nights were very damp and cold. Then, in another surprise, Anthony drove me to the stables and showed me how to hobble Wildfire so that she couldn't wander off during the night. He also warned me to be on the lookout for horse thieves who might see an opportunity in spotting a boy alone camping with a horse. He armed me with a thick leather whip to ward off any troublesome people. He also lent me a pair of saddlebags and a cigarette lighter in case my matches couldn't get a fire going. He advised me to stay within five miles of my first camp and to prevent Wildfire eating certain plants that would be poisonous to her. He also told me to ask permission before crossing private farmland. Finally, he gave me a piece of paper with his name, address and house telephone number on it in case I needed help.

I was extremely grateful for Anthony's help and advice not least of all for allowing me to ride Wildfire. He reiterated that I had been doing him a favour by keeping his horse exercised and fit.

He gave me a huge departing grin and said, by way of goodbye, 'Enjoy your trip because by the time you get back I may well have sold Wildfire.'

I cursed my luck – every time I managed to befriend an animal, I seemed destined to in some way lose it from my life shortly afterwards. This made me even more determined to make the most of my time with Wildfire, who had become quite bonded to me.

On Monday afternoon when I saddled Wildfire for our trip there was a small group gathered at the stables to see me off. It was most unexpected but then people can be amazingly thoughtful at times. There were small gifts of fancy buns and an apple pie, and several contributors, knowing my taste in food, had pitched in to give me a paper bag containing about a dozen little pork pies. The stables had already given me a pair of second-hand riding boots. I was very touched by their kindness but was so embarrassed that I hurried with my preparations to leave as soon as I could. I was not accustomed to receiving presents of any worth from my parents and the kindness of my stable mates made me further realize how odd my upbringing had been.

Anthony's saddlebags proved a boon and I doubt whether I could have managed without them. I had also managed to borrow a slicker, a kind of raincoat that fits over both the rider and the saddle, and so I tied this at the back of the saddle along with a long bag containing my tent, a sleeping bag and one or two cooking utensils. The food was stored in the saddlebags. I had already tried out putting all this baggage on Wildfire and, sweet horse that she was, she did not seem to mind at all. Even so, I could tell that she suspected that something different was about to happen. Waving farewell raised a cheer from the assembled group and for the first time I began to have real forebodings about the wisdom of making this trip. But I was committed now and there was no turning back.

Avoiding the steep bank of the roadway, I headed down the hill towards the river by following bridal paths used by the riding school on its accompanied rides. Wildfire behaved impeccably and seemed to be glad to be enjoying the new vistas. The countryside looked fresh and green after the heavy rainfall of the previous night and the fragrance from the grasses and the trees was born aloft by the gentlest summer breeze. I may have been a young, would-be cowboy, but as I moved on horseback through the trees towards the river in the late afternoon sunlight I was given a true taste of vintage England. I rode Wildfire at a fast trot through the river shallows, over the exposed gravel spits and continued past my choice of campsite just to enjoy the ride amongst the broad-leafed trees in full blossom. We neither saw nor heard another soul, as if the whole world was ours alone to possess and cherish.

I returned to make camp in the protective shadow of the rockface. Having the river to the front and sides lent a reassuring sense of security to my location. I dug a hole in the dry gravel and placed kindling and wood at its base to make the fire. I then raked a deep channel towards the fire-pit to keep it fed with air and I arranged a tripod of thick branches, tied at the apex, over the fire, using it to hang a pot of water. Having closely studied Baden-Powell's *Scouting for Boys* I felt equipped for every contingency. My father would not let me join the Scouts due to some alarms that had been made public regarding incidents of sexual abuse by some scoutmasters, but my Uncle John had given me the book as a guide to camping and survival living outdoors.

Around us, there were patches of fresh green grass for Wildfire to graze upon and I fed her a few horse nuts as a treat for responding so well to the trip. I was aware that some horses would not be happy alone on a ride because the horse is basically a herd animal by nature. She seemed in good fettle and I was happy to fulfil my fantasy of being the lone cowboy travelling alone with his horse through the wilderness. I was in my element. As an orange sunset turned to cloudy gloom I hobbled Wildfire as Anthony had taught me and left her to graze at will. Then I lit the fire and after a brief struggle I soon had a glowing blaze. The salt in the driftwood that I had gathered caused the fire to spit and crackle as if fiery demons were about.

Soon, the lonesome cowboy had less imaginary demons to deal with as a war party of Comanche approached the camp, whooping and yelling. It was five of my friends, fulfilling their promise to join me. Carrying their bikes as they waded across the shallow riverbed, they had arrived in force but turned out to be very friendly Indian warriors, sharing their rations of fish and chips, paid for by indulgent parents, and several bottles of mineral water. No guests could be received with greater joy than these.

Feeding the fire to even greater heights we sat on the ground around it and consumed the welcome suppers. We talked the night away, swapping exaggerated stories. There was a wonderful spirit to our little party by the wild river, and the woods rang out with laughter as mirthful stories were repeated again and again. At last heads began to droop with tiredness and it was time to call it a day. Wading ashore with their bicycles held high, the group of five departed with much merriment and noise.

After they left I was too tired to do anything except stroke Wildfire and bid her goodnight. I crawled into the tent and lost myself instantly in a deep sleep, lulled by the soft murmur of the river. Tomorrow I would be riding out in to the woods again, knowing that whatever happened at home, I would always have the wonder of animals, nature and friendship to help me on my journey.

The night passed without incident to give way to a sweet reveille of birdsong as the first streaks of a yellow dawn penetrated the thin fabric walls of my tent. As the day took hold, the volume of the dawn chorus increased until the wall of sound outside my tent sounded like the bird population's symphony to the rising of the sun. Wearily I responded to nature's morning call to find Wildfire drinking at the river's edge. She raised her head and whinnied hello. I went to her and stroked her magnificent head. Burying my face in her silky mane, with my arms around her neck I told her how wonderful she was and what a great ride we were going to have that day.

Feeding Wildfire a few carrots I'd brought along for her and making do with a simple breakfast of bottled water and some dry biscuits for myself, I broke camp and we were soon ready to move on. The weather was sunny and warm with only a slight breeze as we commenced riding, heading south between riverbanks heavy with foliage. I intended to travel at least five miles upriver before looking for a suitable site on which to make a new camp. I could feel the powerful muscles of my horse's flanks effortlessly thrusting us forwards as we moved deeper into the Derwent Valley. As we wound our way up stream sunlight danced on the river shallows and tall trees creaked as their tops caught the full force of the breeze. The wind made slim branches heavy with late summer foliage fan the air, while butterflies and thousands of tiny insects took to flight. Soon we had to leave the river and follow game trails that wound through the forest. Now and again I would glimpse herds of roe deer browsing amongst the bushes and trees. Startled by our intrusion, they were sent leaping and bounding away in a symphonic dance to escape us.

An eruption of splashing was causing commotion away to our left on the bankside. Reigning Wildfire to a halt I watched through the branches of a tree an otter family – a female with two pups – at play. Shining wet, smoothly contoured bodies were grappling with a trout, no doubt the mother's catch of the morning. The pups shrieked and whistled with sheer excitement to have the big fish in their paws as they played an otter's rendition of pass the parcel. While watching them frolicking and splashing about in the spray that rose up from the whipping of their rudder tails against the river surface, I was reminded yet again that animals also play for fun. Enchanted by their antics and appreciating the independence of their untethered play, I felt a pang of fury against the river authorities who still permitted otter hunts to take place.

Glancing ahead I spotted a belt of green land bordering the river and swiftly heeled Wildfire into the delightful sway of a cantor. At the end of our run I could see that the Forestry Commission had levelled the land and made a picnic area with wooden seats for the general public to enjoy. A group of women and young children were already making good use of the facilities and obviously appreciating the relaxing charm of the riverside bordered by a line of willows. It was time to stop and have a break. I led Wildfire to the river to slake her thirst and then tied her by a short line to a stout fencing post. I loosened her girth so she could also relax. I drank from my bottle of water and ate some of the small pork pies and a couple of cupcakes the girls back at the stables had made for me, and then lay down on the ground to rest. The children playing near their mothers were fascinated by the sight of Wildfire up close and there was much discussion going on about why she was there and what she was doing.

Not far upriver, there loomed the awesome site of the cokeworks where a good number of my father's family, including my paternal grandfather, had found work on their arrival from Ireland. Despite his proximity, I had met my paternal grandfather only once. When I was ten, my father took me to see him because he was very ill and expected to die. I remember an austere-looking man sitting up in bed. The room had a bare appearance as if nobody cared about it. Above the bed there was a large crucifix hanging from a nail in the wall. The only other furnishing was a chair with a torn wicker seat at the bedside, against which rested a walking stick. He wheezed when he spoke, a grim memento of his time working at the coke ovens, and just before we left he placed a bony hand on my head and said, 'Remember to keep the faith.'

I never saw him again. I never met my father's mother, which was a legacy of her refusal to accept my mother into the family even after she had converted to Roman Catholicism. I also fell within the ambit of her rejection, especially as she may have heard the rumour of my true parentage.

Here on this summer's afternoon, such prejudices seemed totally out of place. I wondered if my father's family were ever able to feel the simple joy of looking at a flower or listening to a songbird without feeling guilty or reducing the sensation to a sinful pleasure, which was the impression some of them always gave me. When I reached thirteen years of age, my Aunt Kathleen felt impelled to warn my mother not to feed me too many eggs in case I got some girl into trouble. She once took me aside and advised me in all earnestness that I should go to Dublin to visit the site at the Post Office there where one of my relatives, Rory O'Connor, had been killed by the Black and Tans because he fought for a free and independent Ireland. She seemed weighed down by the bitterness and acrimony of the past as well as her joyless version of religious conviction.

And she was determined to make sure that her own heavy impediments were foisted on the new generation.

Pushing such thoughts aside, I stood and stretched my limbs after lying on the hard ground. The clean freshness of the air made me reflect on the beauty of this area. Nature keeps her most precious gifts for those of us who take time out to pause and think how fortunate we are to live amongst it. England is such a wonderfully endowed heartland of nature. Long may we preserve it. I looked across at Wildfire who epitomized for me the earthy quality of this land and marvelled at the life-force within her. I whistled and she turned her head towards me. I could tell by the look she gave me that she was ready to return to our adventure.

We stepped up the pace as we passed the cokeworks, which were belching flames and foul-smelling smoke. There were rocks now sticking up from the river bed and the water flowed fast over them causing spray to plume into little clouds of vapour hanging over the stream. Riding up the valley became more difficult as the sides became progressively steeper and the tree-growth thicker. As Wildfire was having difficulty negotiating the slippery, uneven terrain, I dismounted and together we scrambled our way up to the top of the hill.

Halting to regain our breath I was able to look over the far side of the hill towards the village of Rowlands Gill in the near distance. Mounted up once more I rode along the ridge until I saw the railway track as it ran along the valley bottom next to the river below us. Soon the hill gave way to an undulating landscape which enabled Wildfire to descend with ease to the valley floor.

We proceeded along a rough track parallel to the river, with the railway on the far side, when without warning we encountered a roughly formed camp of tree branches covered in a ceiling of foliage, in front of which there was a ring of stones bordering a camp fire. The makeshift campsite had been crudely camouflaged by fir-tree branches to shield it from casual view. Squatting by the fire were two unkempt-looking men dressed in shabby clothing. Before I could react one of the men, sporting a ragged beard and wearing long, shaggy hair, jumped up and, spreading out his arms, forced us to halt. Then he began to speak in a dialect that I found difficult to understand. It sounded like normal Yorkshire but was full of old-fashioned words like 'thee', 'thou' and 'wherefore', which gave it a distinctly biblical connotation.

As far as I could gather the gist of what he said was, 'Now, boy, what do you think you are doing riding a horse into private property like that? Get down because there'll be money to pay before we let you go, *if* we let you go. Maybe we'll have ourselves a bit of fun first.'

This last sentence was said with a toothy grin and a sideways glance at his companion who looked equally disreputable and sniggered at the other's words. I felt for Anthony's whip from where I had looped it around the saddlebag. Meanwhile, I felt Wildfire's body go rigid so, as the tramp approached, I pressed my feet firmly down in the stirrups so that I would be ready for anything. The stench from the man was sickening as he came closer and it well may have contributed to what happened next.

Suddenly, with her ears laid flat back against her head, Wildfire bared her teeth and screamed a sound that made the hair rise on the back of my neck and sent me cold all over my body. Then she raised a front leg and smashed a hoof down on the ground with such force that I felt it shudder. The man shrieked and stumbled backwards, tripping over piles of empty bottles and tin cans. Wildfire lunged forward, almost unseating me, and broke through the weak barrier of evergreen fir branches surrounding the site. As we charged past I stared into the eyes of our assailant and brandished my whip as a threat so that he would know what to expect if we ever met up again.

As we galloped through the overgrown bush and tall grasses I slowly reined Wildfire down to a manageable trot and spoke calm words to her while I stroked her neck, easing her back to normal. I rode on a fair distance although I doubted whether there would be any pursuit. Eventually I called a halt as we approached a stream pouring down from the hillside above us. I dismounted and allowed Wildfire time to slake her thirst after all the trauma of the engagement with the tramps. She was lathered in sweat and still trembling a little so I walked her round a small glade to cool her off. I gave Wildfire one of Anthony's salt tablets because she had sweated so much.

Quite suddenly we were confronted by a tall, burly man dressed in green denims and wearing a bush hat. He had a German shepherd dog accompanying him. He introduced himself as the official ranger for the Derwentside Park. When I explained that I was on a camping trip with my horse he asked for my camping licence and I had to tell him that I had no idea that I needed one. He said that the local environmental agency was anxious to preserve the park and its wildlife, and had implemented a policy controlling camping access. He said that a great deal of damage had been caused by campers in the past and told me that a fine of £50 was payable for camping without a licence.

I assured him that it was not my intention to cause damage and there was no way I could pay £50. He scrutinized Wildfire, me and my equipment, and questioned me at length. Finally, he said that he would forget about the licence this time. Then he brought out a map and, handing it to me, pointed out where we were, indicating that about two miles upriver there was an official campsite with shelters, washrooms and showers, and places to light fires and cook food. Since I was just a kid he would forego any fees as long as I camped there, and nowhere else, until the trip was over.

Thanking him for his kindness and advice I informed him about the two tramps further back on our trail and told him how one of them had tried to attack us. Stepping to one side, he unhitched a walkie-talkie device from his belt and began speaking to his headquarters.

He then turned to me, saying, 'Keep to the regular trails and I'll look for you tonight at the camp. We've already had reports about those two and now my colleagues will move in and arrest them.' With a casual wave goodbye he disappeared into the trees and was gone.

The two tramps had blown my confidence about riding and camping alone in the woods, so I was reassured about our safety following our encounter with the park ranger. I stripped Wildfire of her saddle and started to give her a rubdown when she suddenly moved away from me and lay down in the shallow stream bed. She rolled back and forwards in the cool waters whinnying with pleasure and, when she felt contented, she stood up and shook herself, working up a spray that caught the sunlight. I tied her to a tree, giving the rope a good length so she could graze. Then I held her head close to mine and told her how proud I was that she had lived up to her name and protected us both. Back at the stables I would recount the tale of her courage so that everyone there would appreciate that she was a splendid horse. Then I stripped off my shirt and gave myself a quick wash in the stream. After a brief rest it was time to move on and find the ranger's campsite.

All saddled up and refreshed, but eager to stop for the night, we skipped along at a good pace. It wasn't hard to follow the sketch map the ranger had given me and we headed towards the camp, situated in an expanse of valley sheltered between two small hills. Sure enough, just as the sun was sinking towards what promised to be a glorious sunset, I spotted a scattering of huts and an orderly row of tents about half a mile away on the other side of the river to our approach. The river was deep and, being tidal, the currents looked strong enough to sweep a horse off its feet, so I was glad to spot a ford.

We caused something of a stir as we rode up to the gated entrance to the site. A young woman in ranger uniform came out of the main hut and greeted us with a smile. The ranger we had met earlier had passed on the information about us and it seemed that I was something of a celebrity. I was given an official badge to wear and then she opened the gate for us to enter. I dismounted and led Wildfire forward as the ranger directed us to a site well away from the other campers. There was a rustic stone hearth and a flat finely mown surface on which to pitch a tent. Nearby, there were several large heavy stones which could serve as seats. She pointed over to an enclosure where she said kindling and logs for the fire were available and, if we ran out of matches, we could get some from her. There were also washroom facilities behind the line of rental huts. Finally, she mentioned that it would be advisable to keep Wildfire tethered as not everyone among the campers was familiar with horses. Then she wished us goodnight and walked back towards the main area by the gate.

Since we were surrounded by swathes of fresh meadow grass I immediately unsaddled Wildfire, hobbled her and tied the rope firmly around the base of one of the large stones. I fed her some grain nuts and set her to graze while I went to fetch her a bucket of water from a standpipe about fifty feet away. Satisfied that I had done my duty to my mount as any good cowboy should, I then turned attention to my own needs.

With kindling and chunks of ash wood I soon had a fire going. I permitted myself a muted hurray, which Wildfire noted, raising her head and hoarsely whickering with her mouth full of sweet grass. I quickly set out my tent and opened a can of beans, placing it to heat on one of the flat stones of the hearth. I then gathered more wood for the fire and positioned Wildfire's saddle so I could lie down and rest my head by the fire. As I watched the soft evening wind blowing sparks from the fire, I thought my camp was akin to the cowboy style of outdoor living that so thrilled me when I read or watched Westerns. I gingerly wrapped a cloth around the hot tin of beans, which had just begun to sizzle. Setting it aside to cool a little, I lay back on the saddle and allowed my eyes to stray skywards.

The promise of a special sunset had been more than fulfilled. The vista above me was ablaze with light and colour. Streaks of green, indigo and blue opalescence washed over an awesome orange and crimson light. No gods of Ancient Greek lore or even the great artist Turner could have conjured a more magnificent display. Then everything seemed to stop and the sky surprised the onlooker with a final theatrical act in its performance – an explosion of tints and electric shades that made my heart leap with delight. As the sunset colours faded into duskiness I relished my beans and sticks of cornbread, washed down by a bottle of Tizer soft drink that I had brought along as a luxury despite its weight.

I was where I wanted to be and I could not have been happier. I was glad that I had met up with the park ranger who had been both bemused and amused by this a kid of fourteen who had embarked on a solitary camping trip on horseback without precise planning. I think my 'Just mount up and ride out' attitude had struck a chord of empathy in this nature-loving man, and he had discreetly made sure that I was given the protection that such a venture demanded.

Later, just as I was about to turn in, lulled to eye-drooping wooziness by the leaping flames and aromatic fragrance of the fire, the young lady ranger appeared carrying a plate of steak and chips. A camp barbecue had been organized and she had thoughtfully brought me a plate of the leftovers. The sight and smell of the steak suddenly awakened a tremendous appetite in me, brought on by my long day in the saddle in the freshest air that could be breathed. I thanked her profusely and soon demolished the meal.

Whilst I had been eating, the ranger had sat quietly on one of the nearby boulders. Now she came closer and sat by the fire with me. In a friendly conversation that lasted well over an hour she managed to elicit my life story so far, barring any mention of my abusive father. She told me that her name was Sally and that she was from Australia, as was the head ranger I'd met in the woods, who had served in the British Army during the war and had decided to settle here. She had lost her brother and father in the war and, since her mother was already dead, she'd decided to come to England to make a fresh start.

Before she left I felt obliged to dig out three pounds and six shillings, which was all I had, and offer it to her as a token of my gratitude for all the hospitality the rangers had extended to me. The sum was graciously declined. She told me with a smile that the rangers laughingly thought that they had come across a latter-day young Davy Crockett suddenly riding out of nowhere from the Derwentside woods. She said they 'were tickled pink' to see me and couldn't quite believe I was real. As she stood up to leave she mentioned that I could have some of the sketch maps they gave out to the hikers to help me plan a ride and, even better, she would join me on horseback if I wished. She explained that the rangers kept two ponies at the centre in case a hiker got lost in a part of the forest where a jeep couldn't reach.

'If you like, I could show you one of the more scenic trails and we could be company for each other on the ride,' she said.

I readily agreed and thanked her for the offer. At the same time, I wondered if this was the wardens' way of keeping tabs on me in case I got into trouble riding alone. I believed that Wildfire and I could to handle any trouble that came along, but I understood how they felt the need to keep me, a minor on horseback in rough country, under close observation. If anything went wrong they could be held responsible.

I gave Wildfire a last stroke and told her again how wonderfully she had dealt with those two tramps. I then slid into my sleeping bag and checked the time by my old-fashioned pocket watch, a present from my Uncle John which by now had seen better days. It was just after midnight. I listened to the sound of the river coursing its way downstream and the occasional bark and whistle of the local wildlife, but I was soon slumbering away.

In the morning I got up quickly and was soon tackling chores. I never minded doing chores except for the ones I had to do for my father, such as taking his bets to the bookmaker or collecting heavy tea-chests from the Co-operative yard for him to break up for firewood. I didn't so much dislike the jobs he gave me – it was just that he never thanked me or praised me, and treated me as if I was a menial slave. The first job was to refill Wildfire's water bucket and to feed her some of the maize and grain nuts I carried with me. She seemed genuinely pleased to see me and I was treated to some affectionate nuzzling and snorting before she got to work on the horse nuts. It was a real luxury simply to walk over to the washrooms and take a refreshing shower. I didn't have a towel with me so I just dried myself with one of my spare T-shirts.

My fire was a mass of grey ash with just a few red embers but a few careful pokes soon had it blazing again. I had brought along a small frying pan with a collapsible handle and started to sizzle strips of home-cured bacon that Mrs Bramer had given me. I opened another tin of beans and placed it to warm on the hearth while I filled my empty Tizer bottle with water. The morning looked full of promise and after breakfast I washed up, tidied my campsite, stowing away my sleeping bag and cooking utensils inside the tent.

My watch showed ten minutes past nine so I had nearly an hour to wait before joining Sally for the trek on horseback into the forest and hills. Meanwhile, I rubbed down Wildfire, brushed her beautiful mane and saddled her up, ready to move off. I also carefully checked her hooves, something else Anthony had warned me about since the smallest stone lodged in a horse's hoof can turn her lame and unrideable. She looked fine so obviously our little adventure was doing us both the world of good, as my grandmother was fond of saying.

Just as I was finishing combing out the tangles in Wildfire's tail I happened to glance over towards the ranger's hut and saw the young ranger leading a dark brown horse towards us. The horse's name was Tango and he was a four-year-old gelding. The two horses made contact, sniffed each other's identity and then seemed content with each other's company. After a few brief words we were eager to get going and, with Sally leading off, I followed behind. Soon the camp was out of sight and we were riding through thickly wooded terrain on the slimmest of trails, possibly a game trail used chiefly by deer. After a while we emerged on to an undulating plateau covered in gorse and clumps of dark-coloured heather and we were able to ride alongside each other.

I have often found that wildlife is much more tolerant of people on horseback than people walking. We passed stray pheasants and foraging wildfowl, who hardly gave us a second look. Rabbits were numerous in the vicinity of our track and away to our left, as Wildfire noted with an inclination of her head, a herd of roe deer was grazing. Ahead, I could see that we were approaching more trees and soon we were in a forest of older trees with a predominance of oaks and ash. Now and again, we forded powerful streams that cut their way through the forest and led down from the innumerable hills above us to the narrow, hollow vales below.

At one point Sally reined in her horse and pointed down to a beauty spot nestled below us, which she identified for me as Allensford. We avoided the roads that covered the countryside around us but stopped several times to admire the bridges we could see in the distance. Occasionally we could hear the whistles and chugging of the railway trains that travelled through the area. After two hours of fairly gruelling riding we were ready for a break although the horses seemed remarkably fresh. We rested by a glade of willows that graced the banks of a clear stream. After the horses drank their fill, we unsaddled and roped them securely to stout trees. I'd brought some horse nuts for Wildfire, which I shared with Sally's horse. She had brought along a picnic, which included amongst its delicacies some small pork pies, the aroma of which made my mouth water. She'd also brought along a straight-sided flask, the like of which I had never seen, but which fitted more easily into a saddlebag than the rounded variety. It was full to the top with sweet, hot coffee.

We ate the food and drank our coffee in verdant surroundings where, apart from little clouds slowly tracing their way across a clear blue sky, nothing moved. While the horses close-cropped the grass, Sally talked at length about riding. She told me how she had learned to ride on a small farm her family owned in the outback of eastern Australia where she could ride all day and never see another person. She described how wild and open the country was and that it was really easy to get lost or have an accident and no one would ever find you. So it was important to always carry a reliable compass and she showed me hers, a heavy-looking Army model. She looked at me inquiringly then and I felt myself blushing as I admitted I didn't have one. She then proceeded to give me a short lecture on the dangers of camping out in the wild country without taking due care and preparation. She reminded me that the first principle of survival is never travel alone and always leave clear information about where you are going and when you expect to be back. And always, she emphasized this point by raising a finger, carry more provisions than you think you'll need.

When she finished I felt rather shamefaced and admitted to her that my expedition had been severely flawed and seriously dangerous now I looked back on it. She glanced across at me and smiled as a wise older sister might have done. Then she said that she admired the get-up-and-go attitude that you might find in a boy's adventure story but this was real life and if I hadn't encountered the head ranger I could have ended up in grave danger. She made me promise to take more care in future and I said I would. We shook hands on it, which she said was the Australian way to agree something binding.

All saddled up again, we rode downhill along the routes taken by the many brooks and burns as they descended to become part of the river. I needed all my riding competence to cope in places where the downward slope was very steep. Sally turned and gave me a thumbs-up sign after Wildfire and I managed a precipitous bankside where the horse slid right down to her haunches and, but for sheer willpower, I would have been unseated. Riding a horse downhill is a most difficult task – if the horse doesn't panic the rider might and it is a recipe for disaster. I noticed that Sally leaned back and grabbed her horse's tail to steady herself during the descent and I filed that strategy away for future use. Once we reached the valley floor the going became progressively easier and every so often we kneed the horses into a rocking canter that was so intoxicating that it made us both laugh out loud, with only the stony, craggy outcrops that lined parts of the valley and the sentinel trees to witness our delight.

We crossed the ford and rode up to the rangers' station almost before I realized that we had arrived back. Sally said I could bring Wildfire to the stable yard to give her a good wash down with a hose.

Having dismounted she came over to me and said, 'You're invited to have a meal with us all tonight and tomorrow, after you've had a chance to do some birdwatching from our hides, I've volunteered to see you on your way home.'

I realized that I was being taken in hand, but considering how caring and friendly the rangers had been to me I considered it only fair that they would want to make sure that I got home safely without being any further trouble to them.

I dismounted and, taking Wildfire's reins in hand, I smiled at Sally. 'I really appreciate all you have done for me and the way you have directed me. You have allowed me to have the experience I wanted but with your protection, so thank you. I much appreciate your kindness that you didn't send me packing off home that first night.'

She nodded her head with relief and said, 'Well, we were in two minds about that but we admired your initiative even if it was foolhardy. We thought that maybe if you stayed a while with us we could teach you something. Right?'

'Right!' I said.

And on that note we parted to see to the horses and wash up.

'See you around seven-thirty,' Sally called out as she led Tango away.

I walked Wildfire back to my campsite, stripped her of saddle and saddlebags, and then strolled back with her to the stables. Sally had meanwhile washed and rubbed down Tango and now it was Wildfire's turn. I held her gently by her noseband as I turned on the hose and gently sprayed her body with cool refreshing water. She snorted at the first impact of the shower then visibly relaxed as I hosed her down all over. Then I brushed and combed her mane and tail, by which time I was ready to drop with exhaustion. My knees especially were achingly sore.

Back at my campsite I fed Wildfire some horse nuts, filled a bucket for her and, after hobbling her, simply flaked out on top of my sleeping bag and had a much desired siesta. I awoke to the sound of ball games being played across on the grassy expanse near the rangers' station. I walked over to the shower stalls and gave myself an invigorating sluice down after which I discovered that I had a raging appetite.

Since it was already after seven according to my pocket watch, I hung around to watch the preparations for the barbecue. Roast potatoes, heaps of vegetables and fresh salad were being prepared but the main item of attraction was a large piglet that was already speared on the spit, ready for cooking. The charcoal base was just beginning to flame as I walked up and offered my services. I was told that I could help with the serving and general distribution of the food. I saw a sign that said 'Barbecue 5 shillings a ticket' and offered my money, which was politely declined by a female ranger that I hadn't met before. It appeared that everyone knew that I was the kid with the horse and that I was to be a guest this evening.

The barbecue proved a great success. Families collected their food in a spirit of conviviality and gathered in groups to enjoy the al fresco dining. The weather was calm and the river tranquil as it moved slowly past us. After the campers and stray hikers had been served I joined the rangers at a long trestle table and we all ate hungrily of the juicy meat and fried vegetables, which had come from the same local farm as the piglet. I listened avidly to the stories of these men and women who, despite their relatively young age (most of them were in their thirties), had experienced so much. Later, one of the campers started playing a guitar and the singing spread to the whole assembly as the night wore on.

It was dark when I got up to leave. I shook hands with each of the rangers and Sally reminded me that she would show me where the bird hides were in the morning before we left for the journey home in the late afternoon. I nodded agreement and looked across at the big head ranger, who liked to be called Chuck. His face was ruddy and lined in the reflections of the firelight as I expressed, as best I could, how much obliged I was to him. He didn't say anything at first, and just gave me a casual wave of acknowledgement with his right hand. But then, as I was walking away, he called out, 'Come back again and I'll teach you some real bush craft.'

Only I never did ever see him again. Shortly after my adventure the local council closed the rangers' centre due to expense cuts and the wardens were dispersed elsewhere.

Come the morning, after clearing my camp, seeing to Wildfire and using the washing facilities, I made do with a breakfast of plain biscuits and water. I still wasn't very hungry after the barbecue. At ten o'clock Sally came to take me to the bird hides. One was situated in the border of the woodland and the other was cleverly stationed just by the river. There were large information charts pinned to the walls within the huts and she left me to spend some time there. I chose to watch from the woodland hide first and what a find it was. The rangers had hung bird-feeders filled with a variety of bird food and they were in full use. As my eyes grew accustomed to the gloom I could identify, with the help of the charts, a number of birds that I hadn't even known by name before. Over the space of about an hour I had seen black caps, white throats, blue tits, long-tailed tits and bullfinches all frequenting the feeders. In addition, there were numerous goldfinches as well as greenfinches and chaffinches, the latter identifiable by their military-type white flashes along each wing. Once, to my surprise, I saw a great spotted woodpecker, distinguished by his red cap, drumming away at the peanut holders.

Moving on to the hide by the river the viewing was disappointing as far as birdwatching was concerned but I was treated to a flush of blue damselflies swiftly zooming and then hovering above the surface. Then, just as I was leaving, a blue and scarlet streak splashed into the middle of the river and then rose in a veil of spray to fly to a tree. I was convinced that I had just had a brief glimpse of a kingfisher. I was thoroughly satisfied with my birdwatching and, when I met up with Sally again, I didn't hesitate to tell her how impressed I was with the work of the rangers who had set up the hides and feeders. She thanked me and went on to tell me that the rangers bought the bird food with money out of their own pockets, which impressed me even more.

At three o'clock Sally, now riding a sable-coloured gelding called Jonty, sought me out again for the journey home. As we left the centre the other wardens waved us goodbye from the veranda. It had been a wonderful experience and I was sorry to go. I thought that the centre was an amazing place, enabling visitors and schoolchildren to take advantage of the wonders of nature all around. I was enchanted by the setting, which offered everything that I had long yearned for.

It was late summer and some of the trees were already beginning to shed leaves as a foretaste of the autumn to come, but everywhere I looked there were still remnants of nature's summer show. It had rained overnight and the horses' hooves left tracks in the softened earth. Flocks of birds, chiefly siskins feeding on the mature seed grasses, took wing as we approached. There was an unexpected eruption in the calm river surface ahead of us, causing huge splashes of white water. I looked across at Sally we said the same word at the same time, 'Otters!' and laughed together. No doubt the otter family I had seen on my journey up stream were busy fishing and also having fun at the same time.

Gliding past the giant black edifice of the cokeworks, I began to hear the muted sound of traffic on the road to Rowlands Gill, while away to the right was the distant outline of the old railway viaduct. As is so often the case, the return journey seemed so much faster than the outward one, which was full of unknown trails and landscapes to discover. The urban outline of Swalwell soon came into view.

Leaving the trail by the river we halted by the bridle path that led back to the stables. Sally moved her horse alongside Wildfire and reached over to give me a sisterly hug. Barely whispered words of farewell were exchanged and then, turning her horse, Sally was gone. A beautiful episode in my young existence had come to an end, but would be stored forever in my memory.

Back at the stables there seemed to be no one around. Suddenly Amanda appeared and greeted me with surprise. Perhaps sad that I had reached the end of my adventure, I didn't feel like talking much so I said only the minimum and excused myself to take Wildfire back to her paddock. Once there, I groomed her until her coat had a silky sheen. I stored the gear that Anthony had lent me in his shed and left the key with Amanda. She had a message for me: Anthony had sold Wildfire to a man with a pony-trekking business near Ullswater in Cumbria. I was sad and yet happy at the same – sad because I would probably never see her again but happy that she wouldn't end up pulling a milk cart.

With as little fuss as I could manage, I stole away to walk the long route to my grandmother's house. It was a new experience to be using my own legs again and my knees soon started hurting after so much riding so I stopped and removed my riding boots, preferring to walk the rest of the way barefoot.

TAKING FLIGHT

As I tuned back into the everyday world again, I realized that I had made up my mind to do some serious studying because, before too long, I would be taking the new O-level exams, which replaced the old School Certificate. The exams would mark the first and possibly the most important milestone in my future career.

On a cold, dry Saturday morning one October, I took a break from a hard spell of studying to walk along the lonely beach at Tynemouth in order to clear the cobwebs from my mind. It was strange to be without an animal companion in my life, I reflected as I walked on the sand, but I didn't think there would be another opportunity for animal friendship before I left home for good. But then life has a way of soon proving you wrong.

The sea was crashing and roaring, stirred up by a fierce biting crosswind which was reviving my weary frame of mind. Then I saw it. At first I could not work out what it was that lay ahead, blowing about on the sand. Could it be plastic bags and newspapers? I hurried forward, but when I grasped what it was, I really didn't want to know. Flapping about like a piece of garbage in the strong wind was a large bird of some kind. It was hurt, most probably wounded by gunshot. Earlier I had heard the muffled sounds of shotgun fire, probably carried across the water from some wild fowling site on the South Shields end of the coast. The bird grew frantic as I approached. What to do? Numerous possibilities jumped around my mind, The most feasible was just to walk on by. The cold and shock would most likely kill the bird soon enough, or else a dog would quickly despatch it. However, I simply could not leave a wild thing in jeopardy.

Ruefully stripping off my anorak to catch hold of the bird, I finally gathered it in after a few attempts. It was possibly some kind of goose, being too small to be a swan and too big for a duck. I noticed that one of its wings was not working and had blood on it. Carefully securing the bird in my coat, I walked back to the station at Tynemouth as quickly as I could. On the way I spoke softly to it, trying to calm its struggles. No one saw me as I boarded the train for Newcastle, although once on board a couple with children gave me a hard look and then moved seats to be further away.

In Newcastle, I tried to board a bus for Blaydon but the conductor wouldn't let me once she saw I was carrying a big, live bird, which had suddenly started shrieking with pain or fright or maybe both. The passengers who were already on the bus stared aghast at me through the windows. So I started walking. This was not quite the way I had intended spending Saturday but once I had become involved I felt obliged to see it through. My burden seemed to grow heavier with each step I took.

When I was halfway along Armstrong Road, near the munitions factories, I heard a grinding of brakes and a van pulled alongside me. It was a Co-operative painters' van. The men recognized me, having seen me with my father over the years, and invited me inside for a lift. They were a welcome sight even though I had to withstand some ribald comments about the lengths to which I apparently had to go to find something to eat but it was good-hearted humour. When they heard that I was taking my invalid all the way to the Bramers' farm at Axwell Park, they insisted on driving me almost to the farm gates. I gave them a huge thanks and staggered into the yard with my ward.

Mr Bramer came out of a shed exclaiming, 'What you bringing to me now boy?'

In a disused stable I unwrapped my coat which by now was covered in bird droppings. Once loose the bird made a panicky run for the darkest corner of the stall. Mr Bramer shoved his cap back over his head – his usual gesture of bemusement with which I had become very familiar.

'Well now, my lad, I believe you've got yourself a goose and she's in pretty bad shape,' he said. 'There's no doubt about that.'

'What should I do?'

'Well, I think the best we can do for the moment is to leave the creature be. We'll give her some water and leave best alone. Later, if she's still alive we'll see about cleaning that wing but I reckon she's had about as much as she can take and needs rest and quiet. So let's be away.'

In the farmhouse I recounted the tale to Mrs Bramer, who asked if I would call her Florence from now on. She said her husband's name was Gordon, but he liked to be called Bob, the same as his father. Over a plate of liver and onions, we discussed the bird. Bob said he was sure it was a female Canada goose because he had seen flocks of them flying southwards all morning.

'She must have been shot somewhere along the South Shields coast after feeding along the broad mudflats near Roker. She's a fine bird and the morning will tell if she'll survive the shock and the wounding.'

'That was a fine speech from you, no matter,' Florence said to Bob, pressing more food and drink on me.

They wanted me to stay the night but I had to get back to my school books. I said that I'd call round during the week after school finished. Before I left, Florence insisted that I should take a nearly new waterproof anorak that had belonged to Jenny, her daughter.

'Best it has some use,' she said, and in any case she had put my old one on the fire since it was ruined with goose droppings.

It was late afternoon when I arrived at my grandmother's house, and she chastened me for missing lunch time. All was forgiven when I told her the story of the goose.

Studies at school were assuming great intensity as we approached the examinations so it was Wednesday before I had time to call at the farm. What I found there really surprised me. Florence and Bob had worked wonders with the goose, which was now game enough to strut around the yard feeding on whatever she could find and holding her damaged wing out from her side to protect it.

'Me and the missus fettled her right enough,' said Bob. Florence had bathed the bird's wing in antiseptic solution whilst Bob had cut away the damaged flight feathers right down to the follicles in order to encourage new feather growth. 'But she'll need to winter here with us cos it'll take until spring for the new flight feathers to let her fly.'

Having warned my grandmother that there was the possibility that I would be staying the night at the farm, I gladly accepted the Bramers' offer to sleep over. Before dinner I tried to make friends with the goose but she was having none of it. Try as I might, I couldn't get hold of her. Bob chuckled as he watched my efforts and unable to stand it any longer he swooped down on the goose and grabbed her by the neck.

'Take her with you into the shed and get acquainted,' he said, and shoved the goose into my arms.

She flapped around with her good wing, whilst careful to nurse the injured one, and tried her best to escape from my grasp. Inside the outhouse where she was being kept there was an appreciable amount of space furnished with a table and shelves on one of the walls. Once I set her free the goose clambered on to a high shelf and stared at me apprehensively. I had filled one of my jacket pockets with grain before attempting to catch her and now I offered it to her in an attempt to make friends. Making a soft shush-shushing sound I spread some of the grain on the table and stood back and waited. Nothing happened. She turned and looked at me and then at the grain but she never moved from her shelf. Then I tried my old ploy of tenderly talking out my feelings between me and the animal.

'I'd like to pick a nice name for you. How's about Millie? Would you like to be called Millie while you stay here with us and recover?'

I kept this up for another ten minutes during which time she didn't move at all.

For dinner Florence had prepared jugged hare with new potatoes, fresh hand-picked peas and young carrots fried in butter. Whenever I think of the farm that I visited so often in my youth I recall the loving kindness of Florence and Bob Bramer but also the delicious homemade meals, which for me at that time were out of this world. They were simple country fare but they were based on fresh ingredients straight from the field and the soil.

After dinner I ploughed into my school work with determination to do well as the academic route represented my passport away from backstreet poverty, away from my father and away from the prospect of having to take a job with the Co-operative in Blaydon. I had to have a Plan B if I failed to do well in next year's examinations, but all I could come up with was an idea about escaping to London to pursue my love of films, perhaps working as a tea boy for some company like the Rank Organisation.

Meanwhile, each day after school I cycled to the farm to see the goose, who appeared to be thriving. She had quite happily accepted the farm as her home. As well as feeding alongside the chickens and eating the grass bordering the hedgerows, which Bob insisted on maintaining for the wildlife, she was not averse to a swim in the duck pond. I copied Bob's method of catching her, and then would try to stroke her whilst I was holding her. She had a beautifully coloured neck – bottle green with tiny gold and silver flecks. Her eyes were light golden which sometimes turned a slight tinge of green. She got used to me softly stroking her neck and talking to her, telling her how beautiful she was and how I was so glad that I'd been able to rescue her. Sometimes whilst I was stroking her she lapsed into a kind of trance and when I left her she adopted the regular goose sleeping position with her head tucked under a wing. After a few days she started responding more positively to me. Then one evening she at last took grain from my proffered open hand and cackled enthusiastically.

Bob knew all about wildlife and aptly summed it all up for me: 'Each and every animal has its own special ways and they will not be rushed. They need time. We all need time to adjust to something new in our lives.'

Back at the stables, to which I still went at weekends, there had been a crisis. One Saturday night some of the young girl helpers, several of whom were classmates of mine, had organized a party with a horse riding theme and some of them had got hold of jockey outfits. During the celebrations some of the party, who had been drinking cider, began to circulate around the compound. Wildfire was still staying in her paddock before the move to Cumbria, and some of the girls went up to her in the spirit of bonhomie. At the sight of their jockey uniforms Wildfire suffered a sudden attack of fear and rage and started galloping around the paddock, kicking and screaming. Yet when Amanda and Vera, alerted by the girls' urgent alarms, went to investigate, she was just standing there, trembling and sweating profusely, but docile.

When I heard about the incident, which no one at the stable could understand, I immediately linked it to what Anthony had told me about Wildfire's experience at the horse-racing stables where she had been repeatedly beaten. The sight of the jockey outfits must have brought it all back to her. I think Wildfire's memories of being badly beaten were just as vivid as my own.

I telephoned Anthony who confirmed my diagnosis of the trouble. He also congratulated me on having a successful trip with Wildfire and reassured me that the establishment at Ullswater was very professional and that she would be looked after there. He said they were coming for her on Saturday morning and perhaps I'd like to be there. I told him that I wouldn't be able to bear it and that I was going to miss her terribly.

He laughed and said, 'Animals aren't worth getting senti-mental about.'

I replied that I couldn't be anything else and he laughed again, saying, 'Then you're going to suffer a lot.'

'I already have but then I wouldn't have it any other way,' I told him.

'You're a fool, Denis O'Connor, but you're a nice fool. Good luck to you.'

I went to say goodbye to Wildfire on my own. She whinnied and shook her beautiful mane in greeting when she saw me approaching. I hugged and stroked her but for once words escaped me. I fed her two apples I'd brought for her in silence. Then I walked away. I could hear her behind me as she followed me to the fence rails of her paddock and whickered after me but I could not allow myself to turn around.

For months whenever I was at the stables I avoided going anywhere near the upper paddock and refused to listen to any of the accounts of those who had seen her leave. I just stored the memory of her away in the back of my mind together with the family of other animal friends who already resided there. There was nothing else I could do. Someday, when I finally escaped my father's house, I would keep my animal friends close and never feel the necessity to say goodbye. We'd be together for life.

My exam results duly arrived. With shaking hands I opened the plain brown envelope stamped with 'Durham University Examinations Board'. My heart was beating so strongly that I could barely control myself. So many of my hopes and dreams were dependent on these results. Then I saw them typed out in front of me on yellow paper. They were excellent, even outstanding. I sank into a chair and let my breath go with a whoosh. My mother was overwhelmed and became tearful.

'You must go and show your father. He's working at Ebchester. He'll be proud of you.'

I cringed at her suggestion and resisted complying for well over an hour while I allowed myself to bathe in the euphoria of what I had achieved: I would be able to study A levels in the sixth form, hugely increasing my chances of getting on the first rung to a good career. My father was the last person to whom I wanted to show my results but my mother asked again and, for the sake of peace between us, I eventually acquiesced.

I caught the bus to Ebchester with a heavy heart and finally located the workmen's shelter near the Co-operative store where he was working. I remember to this day the look of ghastly surprise on his face when he saw me.

'What do you want here?' he said.

'I came to show you my exam results. Mother thought you'd like to see them,' I said, and tentatively handed him the sheet of yellow paper.

One of the other joiners, who had a son in one of the younger forms, looked over my father's shoulder and whistled aloud when he read the results but my father only handed them back to me with a deadpan face and said, 'Well, you'd best be on your way.'

As I walked away, feeling rather foolish, I head laughter coming from the workmen's shelter. No doubt my father had found something amusing to say about the episode.

On my return, my mother urgently asked me what my father had said.

'He hardly said a word, just as I'd thought.'

She said, 'I'm sure he is proud.'

I couldn't refrain from saying, 'That man will never ever be proud of me and, mother, you know why!'

My mother's face blanched as I spoke but I thought it was time to get things straight. She didn't respond to the opportunity to tell me the truth. She never did.

Entry to the sixth form at Blaydon Grammar School meant that you could count yourself amongst the elite. I revelled in it and was bursting with pride. I was on my way and I knew it. The feeling of competence I'd gained with my O-level results accelerated my efforts to make good at the A levels and was further boosted when my form master said, 'We've decided to enter you for a State Scholarship.'

'What does that mean?' I asked.

'It means that if you pass it well enough there's the possibility of direct entry to an Oxford or Cambridge college with all fees paid and a handsome support grant of nearly £400 annually.'

For a while I was on a kind of high but I had severe misgivings about going to university at either Oxford or Cambridge. As far as I knew these were elitist places where a simple north-eastern boy would not fit in. I decided that I needed time to think about it and meanwhile I had yet to take and pass the necessary exams. Over the next two years I lived to study, which led a woman friend visiting my grandmother to exclaim, 'That boy is suffering from Brain Fag!'

During this time I continued to visit Millie the goose and spend nights at the farm. On one of these visits I finally learned that the real name for the farm was 'Willowbrook Farm'. It had originally been part of the Clavering family's holding at Axwell Park Hall Estate but passed into the hands of old man Bramer during the First World War and had been inherited by the son of the family ever since, passing down to Bob and Florence Bramer. They received constant overtures from developers anxious to build new homes on the site as part of the post-war rebuilding policy, but so far they were determined to resist giving away their farm.

During the winter months Millie began to thrive and Bob remarked on how the new flight feathers on her wounded wing were already apparent. Sometimes she could be seen tentatively flapping her wings after breakfast with the hens. I praised her that evening, telling how she might be ready to rejoin her kind in the spring for the flight back to Canada. I had found out everything I could about Canada geese and discovered, as their name suggests, that they are from the Arctic, Canada and northern parts of the United Sates. Once they mate, they stay together for life. Millie had probably been gathering small fish and shellfish from the coastal mud flats when she was shot. I also read that Canada geese are often referred to as cackling geese. I had already found out why as she always greeted me with a series of high-pitched cackles, which became more pronounced once she spotted the grain in my hand.

After I'd fed her she often came to rest on my knee and I'd stroke her to sleep whilst telling her what a lovely girl goose she was and how much we all loved her. She never fouled my clothing but the shed was covered in droppings, which I had to frequently clean for the sake of hygiene. She loved me to stroke her long neck, with its white chinstrap and the silky green and grey feathers that tapered down to her plump grey body. After a few weeks she had learned to respond to her name, arriving with wing-flapping haste when Florence called 'Millie, Millie' during the morning feed.

I developed a steady rhythm of study in the sixth form and grafted for four to five intensive hours after lessons on most days. More often than not, I spent the time at my grand-mother's house, away from the blubbering of my sisters who were forever whingeing about something or other. When I spent the night at home I had to kneel on a cushion in my bedroom with my books spread out on the bed because the radio was always blaring downstairs so I couldn't use the table in the sitting room.

Sometimes I worked until the early hours of the morning to finish a project and this caused my father's anger to flare up. Whenever he noticed that I was still in bed in the morning he would take the prop – the long wooden pole that was used to hold up the clothes line – and bang it against my window. He could no longer get into my room to tip me out of bed as by then I had fitted a bolt to the door. It seemed that there was to be no respite to his loathing for me.

His dislike reminded me of an ancient folkloric tale that has circulated around the campfires of nomadic tribesmen since before written recorded history began. The story is known throughout Arab lands as the tale of the 'Star Foundling', and emerged out of people fearfully observing the nearness of the red planet, Mars, in the heavens. It's also referred to as the mystery of 'The Baby from Mars'. As told in its original form it describes how aliens from Mars periodically visit Earth to steal newborn baby boys and replace them with babies of their own. The changelings are unwittingly accepted at first but as they develop they become increasingly estranged from their adopted families and may even be rejected by them because they seem so at odds with the rest of the family.

The first time I came across this myth I clutched at it as an apt analogy for my own position within my family. Surely if there ever was such a case then I fitted the syndrome and could rightly think of myself as 'a boy from Mars'.

Work studies at school became increasingly intense as the year wore on and I found time for little else. Christmas brought a round of parties held in other people's homes, but not in our own, where a ragged little pine tree and some Nativity figurines represented Christmas festivity. My sisters did well for presents but, as had become usual, there was nothing for me. However, I would go around to my grand-mother's house where there were always new books and clothes for me, courtesy of Nanna and Uncle John. The Bramers bought me a camera, my first, and I stayed over with them on New Year's Day. At a New Year's Party at Nancy's house I received my first ever kiss and I began to think that life was wonderful. I felt grown up.

I did not apply to either Oxford or Cambridge, which is something I have regretted all my life, but my inferiority complex still had some hold over me. Instead, I applied to Hull University because I had read that a former Oxford don was inaugurating an honours degree course in psychology there, and that was the subject I wanted to study. I was interviewed and accepted on the course, depending on my A-level results. I was advised to gain more experience of life first, so I agreed to do my National Service before taking up my degree studies in October 1955.

As spring approached the Bramers and I were fascinated to watch Millie practising take-offs and landings. Her flight feathers had grown back well and, as we watched her flying around the farmyard, we remarked upon her natural-born resilience and inner sagacity.

Bob said, 'That bird is getting ready to join the spring exodus. She knows, and God only knows how she knows, that it's time to fly to Canada. She's awaiting the call of the wild flocks that will soon be flying overhead and one day she'll join 'em.'

Now, whenever I spent time with her in the shed where she was kept safe from foxes during the night, she was agitated and seemed as if she couldn't settle because the 'call of the wild' was reminding her that it was time to leave and savour again the sights and scents of home. It was my opportunity to view at first hand the power of instinct.

Soon I was yet again involved in the agony of swotting for exams, which made me miss Millie's departure. According to the Bramers it was a late afternoon on a Friday in April. It had been fine, warm and sunny all day when Millie, who was resting on the farmhouse roof, heard the sounds of the flocks calling to each other across the clear blue sky. Florence and Bob heard it, too, as they had done many times in the past. But this year was different because Millie was having an ecstasy of cackling and running about, testing her wings and generally acting very excited. Another 'V' formation was just beginning to come over when she took flight.

'She were as graceful as a big goose can be,' Bob told me. 'Up and up she flew and then something stopped her and she circled back over us calling and calling and it's my opinion that she were looking for you because she knew it was final goodbye time. Even a goose has feelings and that bird had strong feelings for you, we know that.'

I felt like cheering but there was a large lump in my throat. 'Did she make it right up to a flock?' I asked with a tremor in my voice. It was Florence who answered.

'Yes, I watched her through binoculars and she managed to tag on to the back of the V and then I couldn't pick her out any more. You should be proud, you gave her back her life.'

'Only with your help,' I said.

212

'She were a right good 'un and maybe she'll come back to pay us a visit next year,' said Bob, ever the optimist.

Florence looked at me and winked and thus Millie joined the ranks of my absent but dearly remembered animal friends.

The exam results were even better than expected and I wasted no time in informing Hull University. The day I received the letter from Hull confirming the offer of a place I also got my call up papers instructing me to join Six Training Battalion at Blenheim Barracks, Aldershot, on 15 October 1952.

The rest of the summer was spent reading and writing poetry, and walking out with Nancy, who had a place at Leeds University to read English. There was an endless round of parties where my friends all celebrated the end of school and the beginning of a new stage in our lives.

Then the fateful day in October arrived. My mother and my grandmother came to Newcastle station to cheer me on my way. My father, of course, was not there. Nor had he commented upon my acceptance at university. I now knew for certain that we meant nothing to each other and that any effort on my part to gain his approval, never mind love, was fruitless. Both of the women in my life cried and I nearly did as well. I was relieved when the huge train for London King's Cross finally pulled into the station and I climbed aboard and found a seat. As I watched the faces of my grandmother and my mother recede, I decided that I hated goodbyes.

Crossing hectic London by tube I arrived at Waterloo station and immediately felt like a lost country boy in the melée of the busy station. Unsure where to go I approached two surly-looking West Indian porters and politely asked which platform I should be on for the train to Aldershot. One of them turned away from their conversation and said, 'Can't you read, man?'

I was taken aback by his rudeness for a moment, but then something in his words dawned on me. Boyhood was truly behind me. I was eighteen years old. I was a man now and, after what I'd been through, I could cope with anything. I suddenly burst out laughing to the porter's bemusement. Yes, I was a man and I could read and I could find my own way anywhere. The future loomed ahead of me and I was heading into it with full confidence. I knew that I was already on the right path to an independent manhood. So let the future, whatever it held for me, unroll. I was ready.